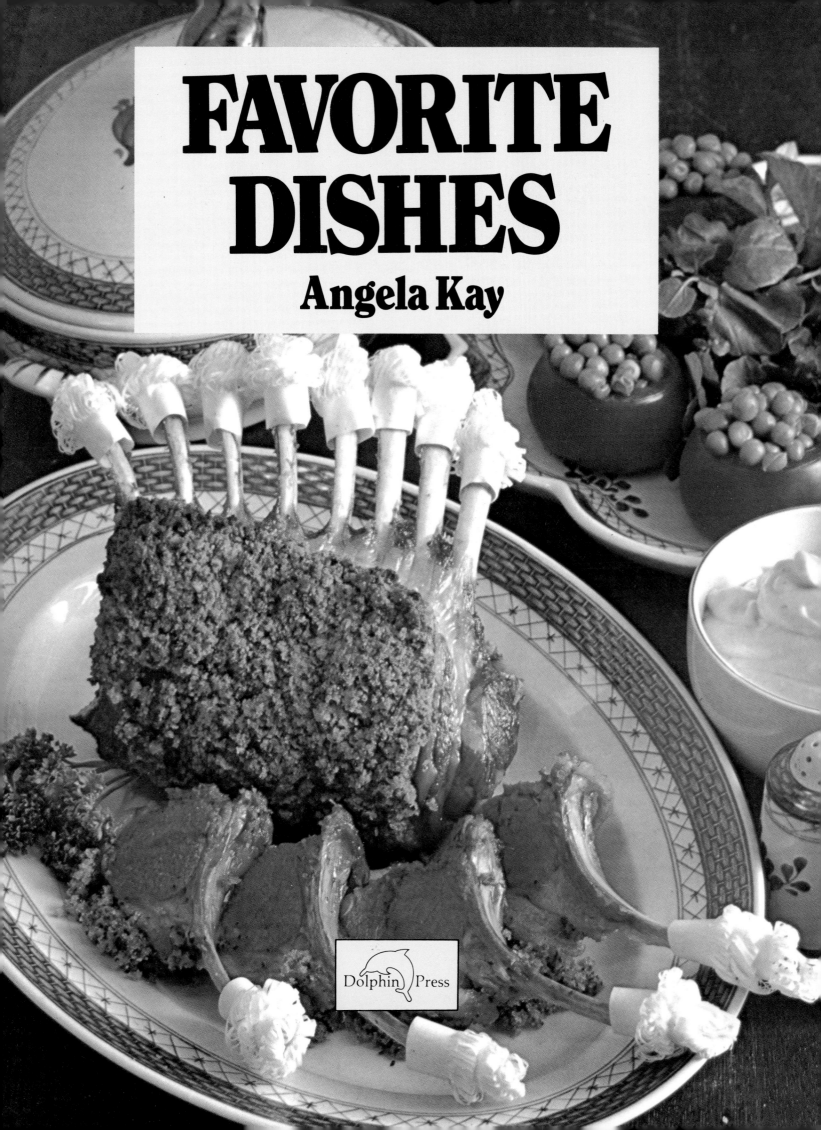

FAVORITE DISHES

Angela Kay

Dolphin Press

First published by Octopus Books Ltd
as *The All Colour Slimming Cookbook*.

This edition published by Treasure Press
59 Grosvenor Street
London W1

© 1978 Octopus Books Ltd

ISBN 0 907407 61 7

Printed in Hong Kong

This edition produced for:
Dolphin Press, 9150 S.W. 87th Ave.,
Suite 108, Miami, Florida, U.S.A.

Contents

Hors d'oeuvre	5
Soups	11
Meat and Poultry	17
Fish and seafood	37
Vegetables	49
Salads	59
Desserts	67
Index	80

Hors d'oeuvre

Tomato and Mushroom Vinaigrette

Metric/Imperial
100 g/4 oz button mushrooms, sliced
100 g/4 oz tomatoes, peeled and sliced
SAUCE:
1 × 2.5 ml spoon/$\frac{1}{2}$ teaspoon made mustard
3 × 15 ml spoons/3 tablespoons corn oil
0.5 × 15 ml spoon/$\frac{1}{2}$ tablespoon lemon juice
0.5 × 15 ml spoon/$\frac{1}{2}$ tablespoon wine vinegar or
  cider vinegar
1 clove garlic (optional)
1 × 2.5 ml spoon/$\frac{1}{2}$ teaspoon salt
freshly ground black pepper
2 × 15 ml spoons/2 tablespoons chopped parsley
  to garnish

American
1 cup sliced button mushrooms
$\frac{1}{2}$ cup peeled and sliced tomatoes
SAUCE:
$\frac{1}{4}$ teaspoon made mustard
3 tablespoons corn oil
$\frac{1}{2}$ tablespoon lemon juice
$\frac{1}{2}$ tablespoon wine vinegar or
  hard cider vinegar
1 clove garlic (optional)
$\frac{1}{2}$ teaspoon salt
freshly ground black pepper
2 tablespoons chopped parsley to
  garnish

Place the mushrooms in a shallow dish. Whisk together the mustard, oil, lemon juice, vinegar, garlic, salt and pepper, or shake them in a screw top jar.

Pour this sauce over the mushrooms and allow to marinate for 30 minutes.

Arrange a layer of tomato in each individual serving dish. Using a perforated spoon, lift out the mushrooms and arrange them on top of the tomatoes. Whisk the sauce again, and pour it over each serving. Garnish with parsley.

Left: Tomatoes and mushroom vinaigrette
Right: Cottage cheese and ham bake (page 6)

5

Cottage Cheese and Ham Bake

Metric/Imperial
225 g/8 oz cottage cheese
2 eggs, beaten
pinch of salt
freshly ground black pepper
50 g/2 oz lean boiled ham, diced
1 × 2.5 ml spoon/½ teaspoon made mustard
7.5 g/¼ oz butter, melted
TO GARNISH:
1 mushroom, sliced
½ green pepper, deseeded with pith removed and sliced

American
1 cup cottage cheese
2 eggs, beaten
pinch of salt
freshly ground black pepper
¼ cup diced lean cured ham
½ teaspoon made mustard
½ tablespoon melted butter
TO GARNISH:
1 mushroom, sliced
½ green pepper, deseeded with
   pith removed and sliced

Blend together the cottage cheese, eggs, salt, pepper, ham and mustard. Butter an ovenproof dish. Pour in the cheese mixture and place in a preheated moderate oven (180°C/350°F, Gas Mark 4) for 20 to 25 minutes, adding the mushroom and green pepper 5 minutes before cooking is complete.

Raw Vegetables with Cottage Cheese Dip

Metric/Imperial
DIP:
0.5 kg/1 lb cottage cheese
1 × 5 ml spoon/1 teaspoon caraway seeds
½ green pepper finely chopped
2 × 15 ml spoons/2 tablespoons finely chopped
   watercress
1 × 2.5 ml spoon/½ teaspoon salt
freshly ground black pepper   1 clove garlic,
crushed (optional)   1 × 2.5 ml spoon/½
teaspoon paprika to garnish
SUGGESTED DIPPERS:
spring onions, trimmed; celery, cut into
strips; radishes, trimmed; carrots, peeled
and cut into strips; chicory leaves;
melon, cut into cubes or balls; olives;
sprigs of raw cauliflower; very young
whole French beans; tiny whole button
mushrooms; strips of green pepper,
deseeded with pith removed; cucumber,
peeled and cut into strips

American
DIP:
2 cups cottage cheese
1 teaspoon caraway seeds
¼ cup finely chopped green
   pepper
2 tablespoons finely chopped
   watercress
½ teaspoon salt
freshly ground black pepper
1 clove garlic, crushed (optional)
½ teaspoon paprika to garnish
SUGGESTED DIPPERS:
scallions, trimmed
celery, cut into strips
radishes, trimmed
carrots, peeled and cut into strips
Belgian endive leaves
melon, cut into cubes or balls
   olives
sprigs of raw cauliflower
very young whole French beans
tiny whole button mushrooms
strips of green pepper, deseeded
   with pith removed
cucumber, peeled and cut into
   strips

Blend together the cottage cheese, caraway seeds, green pepper, watercress, salt, pepper and garlic, sieving (straining) the cottage cheese if a smoother dip is preferred. Pile it into a bowl and sprinkle it with paprika.

Stand the bowl in the centre of a serving dish and surround it with the prepared vegetables.

Below: Raw vegetables with cottage cheese dip

Above: Mushroom salad (page 9)

Normandy Herrings

Metric/Imperial
4 small herrings
1 × 2.5 ml spoon/½ teaspoon salt
freshly ground black pepper
1 large onion, sliced
freshly grated nutmeg
0.5 × 15 ml spoon/½ tablespoon corn oil
2 eating apples, sliced
1 clove
sprigs of parsley to garnish (optional)

American
4 small herrings
½ teaspoon salt
freshly ground black pepper
1 cup sliced onion
freshly grated nutmeg
½ tablespoon corn oil
1½ cups sliced dessert apple
1 clove
sprigs of parsley to garnish
  (optional)

Cut the heads off the fish. Remove and discard the intestines and wash the herrings well in cold, running water. Split each fish along the belly and season them, inside and outside, with salt and pepper.

Simmer the onion in boiling salted water until tender. Drain well and season with salt, pepper and nutmeg.

Stuff each herring with cooked onion, and close them up again. Brush them very lightly with oil and grill for 6 to 8 minutes, turning them during cooking.

Meanwhile, poach the apple and clove gently in boiling water until tender but still firm. Discard the clove. Arrange the hot cooked apple around the herrings and garnish with parsley.

Fish Tips

Whenever possible, buy fish on the day when you intend to eat it. Choose carefully, looking for:
*a fishmonger with a fast
  turnover
*fish with bright, clear eyes
*a clean, inoffensive smell
*fish with firm and springy flesh
*gills of a clear, red colour

Left: Normandy herrings

Above: Melon with smoked ham

Mushroom Salad

Metric/Imperial

225 g/8 oz fresh button mushrooms

SAUCE:

3 × 15 ml spoons/3 tablespoons corn oil
1 × 15 ml spoon/1 tablespoon lemon juice
1 clove garlic, crushed (optional)
1 × 2.5 ml spoon/½ teaspoon French mustard
1 × 2.5 ml spoon/½ teaspoon salt
freshly ground black pepper
1 × 15 ml spoon/1 tablespoon finely chopped parsley

American

2 cups fresh button mushrooms

SAUCE:

3 tablespoons corn oil
1 tablespoon lemon juice
1 clove garlic, crushed (optional)
½ teaspoon French mustard
½ teaspoon salt
freshly ground black pepper
1 tablespoon finely chopped parsley

Wipe the mushrooms with a clean, damp cloth. Leave them whole and do not remove the stalks. Whisk together the oil, lemon juice, garlic, mustard, salt, pepper and parsley, or shake them together in a screw top jar.

Pour the dressing over the mushrooms. Toss them well to make sure that each mushroom is coated with the dressing. Chill, covered, for 2 hours before serving.

Melon with Smoked Ham

Metric/Imperial

1 small melon – Ogen, Canteloup or Charentais
100 g/4 oz raw smoked ham, thinly sliced
freshly ground black pepper
black olives to garnish

American

1 small melon – Ogen, Canteloup or Charentais
¼ lb raw smoked ham, thinly sliced
freshly ground black pepper
black olives to garnish

Chill the melon well before cutting it into the required number of portions. Remove the seeds. Arrange rolled slices of smoked ham on each melon portion. Sprinkle with pepper and garnish with black olives.

Above: Chilled tomato soup

10

Soups

Chilled Tomato Soup

Metric/Imperial
0.5 kg/1 lb stewed fresh tomatoes or canned
   tomatoes
1 × 2.5 ml spoon/½ teaspoon Worcestershire sauce
juice of ½ lemon
1 sliced peeled onion
1 × 5 ml spoon/1 teaspoon salt
4 sprigs of parsley
1 × 425 g/15 oz can condensed consommé

TO GARNISH:
2 × 15 ml spoons/2 tablespoons chopped parsley
2 × 15 ml spoons/2 tablespoons chopped celery

American
2 cups stewed fresh tomatoes or
   canned tomatoes
½ teaspoon Worcestershire sauce
juice of ½ lemon
1 slice peeled onion
1 teaspoon salt
4 sprigs of parsley
1 × 15 oz can condensed
   consommé

TO GARNISH:
2 tablespoons chopped parsley
2 tablespoons chopped celery

Place the tomatoes, Worcestershire sauce, lemon juice, onion, salt and parsley in a liquidizer (blender) and blend until smooth. Stir in the consommé. Chill well and serve garnished with parsley and celery.

Carrot and Watercress Soup

Metric/Imperial
25 g/1 oz butter
225 g/½ lb onions, peeled and chopped
0.5 kg/1 lb carrots, peeled and chopped
1 × 5 ml spoon/1 teaspoon caraway seeds
1 litre/1¾ pints chicken stock
2 × 15 ml spoons/2 tablespoons soured cream

TO GARNISH:
1 bunch watercress, finely chopped
1 carrot, grated

American
2 tablespoons butter
2 cups peeled and chopped onion
4 cups peeled and chopped carrot
1 teaspoon caraway seeds
4¼ cups chicken bouillon
2 tablespoons sour cream

TO GARNISH:
1½ cups finely chopped watercress
½ cup grated carrot

Heat the butter in a thick pan. Add the onions and allow them to cook gently until soft but not brown. Add the carrots, caraway seeds and boiling stock (bouillon). Bring to the boil again, cover and simmer until the carrots are quite tender. The timing will depend on the age and quality of the carrots. Cool soup, then liquidize (blend) and stir in the soured cream.

Serve this soup hot or cold, garnished with watercress and raw carrot.

Minestrone

Metric/Imperial

1 × 15 ml spoon/1 tablespoon corn oil
1 large onion, finely chopped
50 g/2 oz lean bacon, finely chopped
4 celery sticks, chopped
1.2 litres/2 pints beef stock
salt
freshly ground black pepper
225 g/8 oz tomatoes, peeled and chopped
2 × 15 ml spoons/2 tablespoons tomato purée
1 clove garlic, finely chopped (optional)
175 g/6 oz any other diced vegetables in season,
   such as marrow, aubergine, cauliflower,
   cabbage, green pepper (deseeded with pith
   removed), peas or green beans
1 × 5 ml spoon/1 teaspoon fresh basil or thyme

Heat the oil in a large saucepan. Add the onion
and fry very gently, covered, until soft but not
coloured. Add the bacon and fry for a further 5
minutes.

Add the celery, stock (bouillon), salt, pepper,
tomatoes, tomato purée (paste), garlic, diced
vegetables and basil or thyme. Bring to the boil.
Cover with a lid and simmer gently for 45
minutes. Serve very hot.

American

1 tablespoon corn oil
1 cup finely chopped onion
$\frac{1}{4}$ cup finely chopped lean bacon
$\frac{1}{2}$ cup chopped celery
5 cups beef bouillon
salt
freshly ground black pepper
1 cup peeled and chopped
   tomatoes
2 tablespoons tomato paste
1 clove garlic, finely chopped
   (optional)
1 cup any other diced vegetables
   in season, such as squash,
   eggplant, cauliflower, cabbage,
   green pepper (deseeded with
   pith removed), peas or snap
   beans
1 teaspoon fresh basil or thyme

Below: Minestrone   **Right: Bortsch**

Bortsch

Metric/Imperial

1 small onion, thinly sliced
0.5 × 15 ml spoon/½ tablespoon corn oil
100 g/4 oz lean stewing beef (shin or chuck) cut
    into 1 cm/½ inch cubes
900 ml/1½ pints beef stock
1 × 2.5 ml spoon/½ teaspoon salt
freshly ground black pepper
½ bay leaf
1 × 5 ml spoon/1 teaspoon chopped fresh thyme,
    or
1 × 2.5 ml spoon/½ teaspoon dried thyme
1 clove garlic, finely chopped (optional)
1 small carrot, thinly sliced
¼ small turnip, thinly sliced
⅛ cabbage, finely shredded
1 large tomato, peeled and chopped
1 large beetroot, peeled and grated
4 × 5 ml spoons/4 teaspoons soured cream to
    garnish

American

½ cup thinly sliced onion
½ tablespoon corn oil
¼ lb lean stewing beef (shin or
    chuck) cut into ½ inch cubes
3¾ cups beef bouillon
½ teaspoon salt
freshly ground black pepper
½ bay leaf
1 teaspoon chopped fresh thyme,
    or
½ teaspoon dried thyme
1 clove garlic, finely chopped
    (optional)
¼ cup thinly sliced carrot
¼ cup thinly sliced turnip
½ cup finely shredded cabbage
¼ cup peeled and chopped tomato
2 cups peeled and grated beet
4 teaspoons sour cream to garnish

Fry the onion slowly in the oil, in a thick pan. When golden brown, add the meat. Toss it well over the heat until each cube of meat is brown all over. Add the stock (bouillon), salt, pepper, bay leaf, thyme and garlic. Cover the pan, bring to the boil, then reduce the heat and allow to simmer for 5 minutes. Add the carrot, turnip and cabbage, return to the boil and simmer for 45 minutes. Add the tomato and simmer for a further 20 minutes. Add the grated beetroot (beet) 5 minutes before serving. Check the seasoning and top each portion with a spoonful of soured cream.

Above: Chilled
summer soup

Iced Spanish Soup

Metric/Imperial

0.75 kg/1½ lb tomatoes, skinned, deseeded and
  chopped
10 cm/4 inch cucumber, chopped
 3 spring onions, chopped
   ½ green pepper, deseeded with pith removed and
     chopped
   2 cloves garlic
   4 × 15 ml spoons/4 tablespoons corn oil
   1.5 × 15 ml spoons/1½ tablespoons cider vinegar
   1 × 5 ml spoon/1 teaspoon fresh thyme or parsley
   salt
freshly ground black pepper
iced water

TO GARNISH:
ice cubes
½ green pepper, deseeded with pith removed and
   finely diced
10 cm/4 inch cucumber, finely chopped
4 sticks celery, finely chopped
finely chopped parsley

American

3 cups skinned, deseeded and
   chopped tomatoes
¾ cup chopped cucumber
½ cup chopped scallions
½ cup chopped green pepper,
   deseeded with pith removed
2 cloves garlic
¼ cup corn oil
1½ tablespoons hard cider vinegar
1 teaspoon fresh thyme or parsley
salt
freshly ground black pepper
iced water

TO GARNISH:
ice cubes
½ cup finely diced green pepper,
   deseeded with pith removed
¾ cup finely chopped cucumber
½ cup finely chopped celery
finely chopped parsley

Blend together the tomatoes, cucumber, spring
onions (scallions), green pepper, garlic, oil, cider
vinegar, thyme, salt and pepper in a liquidizer
(blender).

Add enough iced water to make the soup of the
desired consistency. The quantity will vary
according to the juiciness of the tomatoes, and
your preference for a really thick or a thin soup.

Chill thoroughly. Float an ice cube in each
serving and hand round the garnishes separately.

Chilled Summer Soup

Metric/Imperial

1 small onion, chopped
900 ml/1½ pints chicken stock
½ cucumber, chopped but unpeeled
1 bunch watercress
1 small lettuce, shredded
sprig of mint
pinch of salt
freshly ground black pepper
2 × 15 ml spoons/2 tablespoons soured cream
2 × 15 ml spoons/2 tablespoons finely chopped
   pickled gherkin to garnish

American

½ cup chopped onion
3¾ cups chicken bouillon
1 cup unpeeled, chopped
   cucumber
1 bunch watercress
1½ cups shredded lettuce
sprig of mint
pinch of salt
freshly ground black pepper
2 tablespoons sour cream
2 tablespoons finely chopped dill
   pickle to garnish

Place the onion and chicken stock in a saucepan
and bring to the boil. Reduce the heat and allow to
simmer for 10 minutes. Add the cucumber,
watercress, lettuce and mint. Simmer for a further
7 minutes. Cool. Blend the soup in a liquidizer
(blender) until quite smooth. When cold, stir in
the soured cream. Chill well, and garnish with
gherkins (dill pickles) just before serving.

Watermelon Soup

Metric/Imperial

25 g/1 oz dried mushrooms, chopped
600 ml/1 pint chicken stock
175 g/6 oz chicken, minced
175 g/6 oz lean pork, minced
100 g/4 oz bamboo shoots, thinly sliced
100 g/4 oz lean ham, minced
100 g/4 oz green peas
1 × 1.75 kg/4 lb watermelon

American

$\frac{1}{4}$ cup chopped dried mushrooms
$2\frac{1}{2}$ cups chicken bouillon
$\frac{3}{4}$ cup ground chicken
$\frac{3}{4}$ cup ground lean pork
$\frac{2}{3}$ cup bamboo shoots, thinly sliced
$\frac{1}{2}$ cup ground lean ham
$\frac{3}{4}$ cup green peas
1 × 4 lb watermelon

Pour boiling water over the mushrooms and allow them to soak for 1 hour. Drain them well.

Bring the stock (bouillon) to the boil. Add the chicken and pork and simmer for 10 minutes. Add the drained mushrooms, bamboo shoots, ham and peas.

Cut the top from the melon. Scoop out the seeds and some of the pulp. Pour the soup into the melon and replace the top.

Stand the melon in a heatproof basin and steam it, in or over a large pan of boiling water for about $1\frac{1}{2}$ hours or until the melon is cooked.

The correct way to serve this soup is to place the melon on the table and scoop out melon flesh as well as soup for each serving. Cut down the peel as the level of soup is lowered.

Below:
Watermelon soup

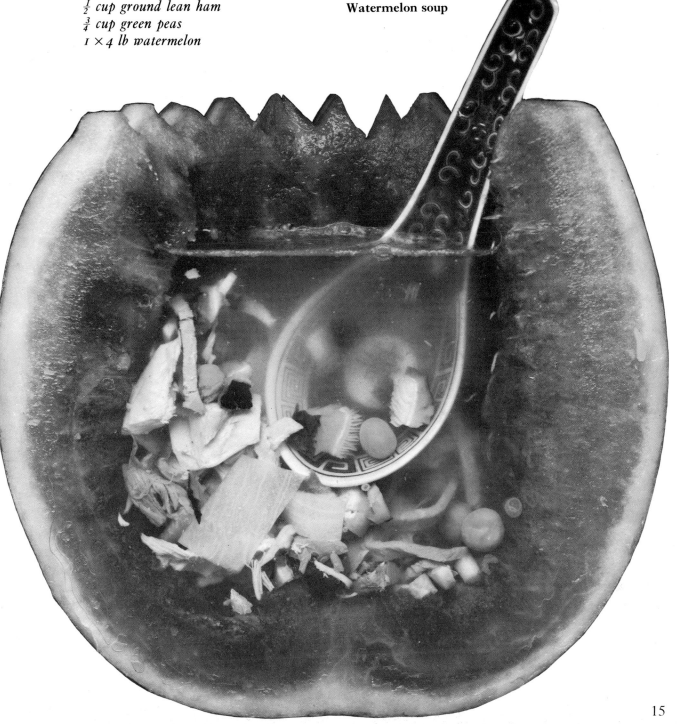

15

Cold fillet of beef (Roast beef, page 17)

Meat and poultry

Beef with Cabbage

Metric/Imperial
0.5 kg/1 lb rump steak
1 clove garlic, crushed
1 × 15 ml spoon/1 tablespoon corn oil
2 sticks celery, cut into strips
4 spring onions, finely chopped
100 g/4 oz white cabbage, shredded
1 × 15 ml spoon/1 tablespoon soya sauce
salt
freshly ground black pepper

American
1 lb rump steak
1 clove garlic, crushed
1 tablespoon corn oil
2 stalks celery, cut into strips
4 scallions, finely chopped
1½ cups shredded white cabbage
1 tablespoon soya sauce
salt
freshly ground black pepper

Wipe the meat and rub with crushed garlic. Cut into paper thin slices, then into small strips.

Heat the oil in a frying pan (skillet) and fry the meat over a very fierce heat for 3 minutes, stirring all the time. Remove the meat from the pan.

Add the celery, spring onions (scallions), and cabbage to the remaining fat in the pan and fry gently for 5 minutes, stirring occasionally.

Return the meat to the pan and add the soya sauce, salt and pepper. Mix well and cook for 2 to 3 minutes. Serve immediately.

Roast Beef

Choose a prime cut of beef for roasting, either sirloin, rib, Chateaubriand or good quality topside (top round). You will need no additional fat when roasting sirloin or rib, but brush a Chateaubriand or topside (top round) with just a little oil or melted butter to keep it succulent.

Place the seasoned meat – plain, studded with garlic or strewn with herbs – in an open roasting pan, then place the pan in a preheated hot oven (220°C/425°F, Gas Mark 7) and cook for 20 minutes, to seal the outside of the meat. Reduce the temperature to 190°C/375°F, Gas Mark 5.

If you like beef underdone allow 15 minutes per lb plus an extra 15 minutes; if you prefer it well done, allow 20 minutes per lb plus an extra 20 minutes. For an extremely small joint, say 2 lb, be a little generous with your timings.

Accompany your roast beef with a mixed, fresh green salad of celery, watercress, lettuce, chicory (Belgian endive) and cucumber. Horseradish sauce and mustard are traditional partners for roast beef. Serve the meat juices separately, not thickened of course, but spiced if you prefer.

Slimmers' Stroganoff

Metric/Imperial
0.5 kg/1 lb good quality stewing beef
15 g/½ oz butter
2 medium onions, finely chopped
100 g/4 oz mushroom, sliced
salt
freshly ground black pepper
pinch of nutmeg
1 × 2.5 ml spoon/½ teaspoon basil
150 ml/¼ pint stock
300 ml/½ pint natural yogurt
2 × 15 ml spoons/2 tablespoons soured cream
chopped parsley or chives to garnish

American
1 lb good quality stewing beef
1 tablespoon butter
1 cup finely chopped onion
1 cup sliced mushrooms
salt
freshly ground black pepper
pinch of nutmeg
½ teaspoon basil
⅔ cup beef bouillon
1¼ cups unflavored yogurt
2 tablespoons sour cream
chopped parsley or chives to garnish

Cut the meat into thin slices and then into strips, like thick matchsticks. Heat the butter in a pan, add the onions and sauté them until transparent. Add the meat and brown over a fairly high heat. When each piece of meat is brown all over, reduce the heat and add the mushrooms, salt, pepper, nutmeg, basil and stock (bouillon).

Bring to the boil, then cover and simmer for 40 to 45 minutes. Stir in the yogurt and soured cream.

Check the seasoning and reheat, without allowing it to boil. Sprinkle with parsley or chives before serving.

Meat Tips

Meat is too expensive to make mistakes with, so be sure that you have meat which has been properly hung and butchered, and which is the appropriate cut for the recipe which you have chosen. This means patronizing a reliable butcher.

Tougher cuts of meat can always be made more tender – and more tasty – by soaking in a marinade for several hours before cooking. Marinades usually contain a little oil, some wine, lemon juice or vinegar, herbs and seasonings.

Left: Slimmers' Stroganoff

French Country Casserole

Metric/Imperial
15 g/½ oz butter
1 × 15 ml spoon/1 tablespoon corn oil
12 small onions or shallots
2 cloves garlic, chopped
1 kg/2 lb topside steak, cut into 2.5 cm/1 inch
    cubes
225 g/8 oz tomatoes, peeled and chopped
1 × 15 ml spoon/1 tablespoon tomato purée
pinch of cinnamon
salt
freshly ground black pepper
450 ml/¾ pint beef stock
100 g/4 oz mushrooms, sliced
2 × 15 ml spoons/2 tablespoons lemon juice

American
1 tablespoon butter
1 tablespoon corn oil
12 small onions or shallots
2 cloves garlic, chopped
2 lb top round of beef, cut into 1
    inch cubes
1 cup peeled and chopped
    tomatoes
1 tablespoon tomato paste
pinch of cinnamon
salt
freshly ground black pepper
2 cups beef bouillon
1 cup sliced mushrooms
2 tablespoons lemon juice

Heat the butter and oil in a flameproof casserole. Fry the peeled onions and garlic in this until golden all over. Remove them from the pan and set aside.

Fry the cubed beef until brown all over. Remove it from the pan and set aside.

Fry the tomatoes until they start to soften. Stir in the tomato purée (paste), cinnamon, salt, pepper and stock (bouillon). Bring to the boil, add the meat, onions and garlic. Return to the boil, cover and cook in a preheated moderate oven (160°C/325°F, Gas Mark 3) for 1½ to 2 hours.

Sprinkle the mushrooms with lemon juice, and add them to the casserole 15 minutes before cooking is complete.

Pepper Steak

Metric/Imperial
4 steaks, fillet or rump
0.5 × 15 ml spoon/½ tablespoon corn oil
3 × 5 ml spoons/3 teaspoons whole black
    peppercorns

American
4 steaks, fillet or rump
½ tablespoon corn oil
3 teaspoons whole black
    peppercorns

Trim the steaks neatly. Beat them with a steak mallet or rolling pin to tenderize. Paint each one, on both sides, with oil.

Crush the peppercorns coarsely with a rolling pin. Press these into the steaks on both sides and allow to stand for 1 hour.

Preheat the grill (broiler) at its maximum temperature for 5 minutes before grilling (broiling) the steaks quickly on both sides to seal in the juices. Then reduce the heat and cook according to taste – rare, medium or well done.

Left: French country casserole

19

Boiled Salt Silverside (Brisket), or Ox (Beef) Tongue

You have to plan ahead when you are cooking salted meat It must be soaked in cold water for at least 12 hours before cooking; longer still if you know it to be heavily brined or if you wish it to be particularly mild.

When the meat has soaked for the required length of time, throw away the soaking water. Choose a large pan for cooking. This will allow the liquid to surround the meat completely, otherwise it might become dry and cooking might be uneven.

Put the soaked meat in the pan together with whatever chopped or sliced vegetables you choose – celery, onions, carrots, leeks. Cover generously with fresh, cold water, flavoured perhaps with a little lemon or orange juice. Do not add salt, but a few black peppercorns, some slivers of orange or lemon peel and a bouquet garni would make flavourful additions.

Bring to the boil, removing any scum from the surface as it rises. Then simmer gently, allowing 25 to 30 minutes per lb, plus an extra 25 to 30 minutes.

Boiled salt beef may be served hot, with its accompanying vegetables. Alternatively, if it is to be served cold, it should be allowed to cool in the liquid, then sliced neatly and served with a selection of salads and fairly sharp tasting pickles. Beetroot (beet), red cabbage, gherkins (dill pickle) and horseradish marry happily with cold salt beef. A choice of mustards – French, German and English – will be appreciated too.

Cold Baked Silverside (Brisket) of Beef

Metric/Imperial

1.25–1.5 kg/2½–3 lb silverside of beef, or top sirloin roast, salted
1 carrot, roughly chopped
1 onion, roughly chopped
1 clove garlic, crushed
1 bay leaf
6 black peppercorns
2 cloves
120 ml/4 fl oz brown ale, bottled

American

2½–3 lb brisket of beef, or top sirloin roast, salted
¾ cup roughly chopped carrot
¾ cup roughly chopped onion
1 clove garlic, crushed
1 bay leaf
6 black peppercorns
2 cloves
½ cup dark beer, bottled

Soak the salted beef in cold water for 12 hours. Drain it, and place it in a flameproof casserole with the carrot, onion, garlic, bay leaf, peppercorns, cloves and brown ale (dark beer).

Add sufficient water to cover the beef. Bring to the boil, cover with a lid and cook in a preheated moderately low oven (150°C/300°F, Gas Mark 2) for 2½ to 3 hours, or until tender. Test by inserting a skewer or fork; it should come out easily if the meat is cooked.

Transfer the cooked beef to a large bowl. Cover it with a plate or board, resting on the meat. Cover with a heavy weight. Leave to stand, overnight if possible.

Serve cold and sliced.

Instead of preparing several different salads to serve with the Cold Baked Silverside (Brisket), make one large but very varied salad. An Israeli Salad would be suitable, with lettuce, green pepper (deseeded with pith removed), cucumber, tomatoes, spring onions (scallions), and soft-boiled (soft-cooked) eggs, whose yolks mingle with an oil and lemon dressing.

Or a Salade Niçoise could be prepared or a mixture of diced cooked French beans, leeks, parsnips, broccoli with some sliced raw mushrooms and onions all blended in a herb and yogurt dressing.

Left: Boiled salt silverside (brisket)

Above: Cold baked silverside (brisket) of beef

Spiced Simmered Leg of Lamb

Above: Spiced simmered leg of lamb

Metric/Imperial

1.5 kg/3 lb leg (or shoulder) of lamb
1 × 5 ml spoon/1 teaspoon salt
1 × 15 ml spoon/1 tablespoon soya sauce
1 × 15 ml spoon/1 tablespoon lemon juice
2 cloves garlic, crushed
25 g/1 oz green ginger, shredded or 1 × 5 ml
  spoon/1 teaspoon ground ginger
1 × 15 ml spoon/1 tablespoon corn oil
1.2 litres/2 pints mild stock, vegetable or chicken

American

3 lb leg (or shoulder) of lamb
1 teaspoon salt
1 tablespoon soya sauce
1 tablespoon lemon juice
2 cloves garlic, crushed
1 oz green ginger, shredded or 1
  teaspoon ground ginger
1 tablespoon corn oil
5 cups bouillon, vegetable or chicken

Wipe the meat and rub salt into the skin. Put it into a pan with enough cold water to cover. Bring to the boil and remove the scum from the surface with a perforated spoon. Cover the pan and allow to simmer for 20 minutes. Drain off the liquid.

Blend together the soya sauce, lemon juice, garlic and ginger. Rub the lamb with this mixture and allow it to stand for at least 10 minutes.

Heat the oil and fry the lamb quickly until brown all over. Add the stock (bouillon), bring to the boil, cover and simmer for 2½ hours. Transfer the lamb to a serving dish and keep it hot.

Boil the liquid over a fierce flame until well reduced, and serve this separately.

Lamb Shish Kebabs with Herbs

Metric/Imperial

SAUCE:

250 ml/8 fl oz tomato juice
2 × 5 ml spoons/2 teaspoons prepared mustard
300 ml/½ pint natural yogurt
pinch of cayenne pepper
2 × 5 ml spoons/2 teaspoons finely chopped mint
2 × 5 ml spoons/2 teaspoons finely chopped chives
    or spring onions
salt
freshly ground black pepper
0.5 × 2.5 ml spoon/¼ teaspoon ground cinnamon

KEBABS:

0.5 kg/1 lb lean lamb (from the leg), cut into
    2.5 cm/1 inch cubes
1 green pepper, deseeded with pith removed
    and cut into 8 pieces
12 button mushrooms
4 small tomatoes, halved
12 pickling onions
1 × 15 ml spoon/1 tablespoon corn oil
salt
freshly ground black pepper

American

SAUCE:

1 cup tomato juice
2 teaspoons prepared mustard
1¼ cups unflavored yogurt
pinch of cayenne pepper
2 teaspoons finely chopped mint
2 teaspoons finely chopped chives
    or scallions
salt
freshly ground black pepper
¼ teaspoon ground cinnamon

KEBABS:

1 lb lean lamb (from the leg) cut
    into 1 inch cubes
1 green pepper, deseeded with
    pith removed and cut into 8
    pieces
12 button mushrooms
4 small tomatoes, halved
12 pickling onions
1 tablespoon corn oil
salt
freshly ground black pepper

In a shallow dish mix together the tomato juice, mustard, yogurt, cayenne pepper, mint, chives, salt, pepper and cinnamon. Marinade the lamb in this sauce for 3 to 4 hours, turning it occasionally.

Thread the meat, pepper, mushrooms, tomatoes and onions alternately on 4 long metal skewers. Brush the vegetables with oil.

Season the kebabs lightly with salt and pepper. Cook under a hot grill (broiler), or on a barbecue, turning several times and basting with the sauce. Heat the remaining sauce and serve it separately.

Right: Lamb shish kebabs with herbs

Lamb Casserole with Orange

Metric/Imperial

MARINADE:

4 × 15 ml spoons/4 tablespoons fresh orange juice
2 × 5 ml spoons/2 teaspoons grated orange rind
1 × 5 ml spoon/1 teaspoon ground ginger
salt
freshly ground black pepper

1 kg/2 lb lean lamb, diced
0.5 × 15 ml spoon/½ tablespoon corn oil
1 large onion, chopped
150 ml/¼ pint chicken stock

American

MARINADE:

¼ cup fresh orange juice
2 teaspoons grated orange rind
1 teaspoon ground ginger
salt
freshly ground black pepper

2 lb lean lamb, diced
½ tablespoon corn oil
1 cup chopped onion
⅔ cup chicken bouillon

Blend together the orange juice, orange rind, ginger, salt and pepper. Allow the meat to soak in this for at least 2 hours, turning it from time to time. Remove the meat carefully from the marinade and wipe it with kitchen paper.

Brush a frying pan (skillet) with the oil and when hot, toss the meat in this quickly until brown all over. Transfer it to a casserole.

Fry the chopped onion quickly until golden and add it to the meat.

Pour the marinade into the frying pan (skillet), add the stock and bring to the boil. Pour this over the meat and cook in a preheated moderate oven (160°C/325°F, Gas Mark 3) for 2 to 2½ hours.

Minced Veal Escalopes

Metric/Imperial

0.5 kg/1 lb minced veal
1 clove garlic, crushed
juice and grated rind of ½ lemon
2 × 5 ml spoons/2 teaspoons salt
1 egg, beaten
3 × 15 ml spoons/3 tablespoons corn oil
120 ml/4 fl oz beef stock

American

2 cups (firmly packed) ground
  veal
1 clove garlic, crushed
juice and grated rind of ½ lemon
2 teaspoons salt
1 egg, beaten
3 tablespoons corn oil
½ cup beef bouillon

Blend together the veal, garlic, lemon juice, lemon rind, salt and egg. Form the mixture into 8 balls of equal size. Allow them to stand in a cool place for 1 hour, then roll them out to a thickness of 1 cm/½ inch.

Heat the oil and when really hot, add the minced escalopes. Cook for 2 minutes on each side. Add the stock (bouillon) and allow to simmer gently for 10 to 12 minutes.

Piquant Veal Escalopes (Scallops)

Metric/Imperial

4 escalopes of veal
salt
freshly ground black pepper
1 lemon
25 g/1 oz butter
6 spring onions
2 × 5 ml spoons/2 teaspoons rosemary
0.5 × 2.5 ml spoon/¼ teaspoon Tabasco

American

4 scallops of veal
salt
freshly ground black pepper
1 lemon
2 tablespoons butter
6 scallions
2 teaspoons rosemary
¼ teaspoon Tabasco

Flatten the escalopes (scallops) with a steak mallet or rolling pin. Cut each thin escalope (scallop) in half. Season them with salt, pepper and the juice of ½ lemon.

Heat the butter in a frying pan (skillet). When the butter is foamy put in the meat and fry it until golden, turning each piece once. Remove from the pan (skillet) and keep the meat hot.

In the same pan (skillet) fry the chopped white part of the spring onions (scallions) until soft. Replace the veal and add the rosemary and Tabasco and the thinly sliced lemon half. Cook for 2 to 3 minutes, then sprinkle with the finely chopped green part of the spring onions (scallions) before serving.

Above: Piquant veal escalopes (scallops)

Above: Chicken with bacon and mushrooms

Chicken with Bacon and Mushrooms

Metric/Imperial
1 × 1.5 kg/3–3½ lb roasting chicken
15 g/½ oz butter
100 g/4 oz lean bacon, diced
100 g/4 oz button mushrooms, halved
12 small onions or shallots
300 ml/½ pint chicken stock
juice of ½ lemon
bouquet garni

American
1 × 3–3½ lb roasting chicken
1 tablespoon butter
½ cup diced lean bacon
1 cup halved button mushrooms
12 small onions or shallots
1¼ cups chicken bouillon
juice of ½ lemon
bouquet garni

Cut the chicken into four portions. Heat the butter in a frying pan (skillet) and fry the chicken pieces until lightly browned all over. Transfer them to a casserole.

Fry the bacon, mushrooms and onions for 4 to 5 minutes, then add them to the chicken.

Pour the stock (bouillon) and lemon juice into the frying pan (skillet) and bring to the boil, stirring well to incorporate all the juices left by the chicken, bacon and vegetables. When boiling, pour this over the chicken. Add the bouquet garni. Cover, and cook in a preheated moderate oven (160°C/325°F, Gas Mark 3) for 1 hour.

Check the seasoning, and discard the bouquet garni before serving.

Chicken Veronica

Metric/Imperial
4 × 15 ml spoons/4 tablespoons dry white wine
2 × 15 ml spoons/2 tablespoons corn oil
juice of ½ lemon
225 g/½ lb grapes, peeled, halved and deseeded
1 cooked chicken (approximately 1.5 kg/3 lb)
1 lettuce, washed and shredded

American
¼ cup dry white wine
2 tablespoons corn oil
juice of ½ lemon
2 cups peeled, halved and de-seeded grapes
1 cooked chicken (approximately 3 lb)
1 head lettuce, washed and shredded

Boil the wine in a small pan until reduced by half. Add the oil, lemon juice and grapes. Mix well and allow to cool.

Cut the chicken into neat pieces, discarding any skin or bones. Toss together the chicken, lettuce and grape dressing before serving.

Chicken with Peppers

Metric/Imperial

1 × 15 ml spoon/1 tablespoon corn oil
1 large onion, chopped
1 green pepper, deseeded with pith removed and
    cut into rings
2 red peppers, deseeded with pith removed and
    cut into rings
1 × 5 ml spoon/1 teaspoon salt
4 × 15 ml spoons/4 tablespoons fresh orange juice
0.5 kg/1 lb cooked chicken, cut into 2.5 cm/
    1 inch pieces
pinch of cinnamon

American

1 tablespoon corn oil
½ cup chopped onion
1 green pepper, deseeded with
    pith removed and cut into
    rings
2 red peppers, deseeded with pith
    removed and cut into rings
1 teaspoon salt
¼ cup fresh orange juice
2 cups roast chicken, cut into 1
    inch pieces
pinch of cinnamon

Brush a frying pan (skillet) with the oil. Heat it and add the onion. Cook gently until soft but not brown. Add the peppers and salt and fry for 1 minute.

Pour in the orange juice, bring to the boil, cover and allow to simmer for 2 minutes.

Stir in the chicken and cinnamon and simmer for a further 5 minutes, or until thoroughly heated. Check the seasoning before serving.

Above: Chicken with peppers

Above: Chicken and peach salad

Chicken and Peach Salad

Metric/Imperial

1 small or ½ large cold roast chicken
1 lettuce
1 head chicory
few sprigs watercress
1 ripe pear, cut into 8 pieces
2 ripe peaches, peeled and sliced, or 1 × 0.5 kg/
  1 lb can sliced peaches
3 × 15 ml spoons/3 tablespoons lemon juice
12 black grapes, seeded
slice of lemon to garnish

SAUCE:
225 g/8 oz cottage cheese
2 × 15 ml spoons/2 tablespoons lemon juice
salt
freshly ground black pepper
pinch of paprika

American

1 small or ½ large cold roast
  chicken
1 head lettuce
1 head Belgian endive
few sprigs watercress
1 ripe pear, cut into 8 pieces
2 ripe peaches, peeled and sliced,
  or 1 × 1 lb can sliced peaches
3 tablespoons lemon juice
12 purple grapes, pitted
slice of lemon to garnish

SAUCE:
1 cup cottage cheese
2 tablespoons lemon juice
salt
freshly ground black pepper
pinch of paprika

Cut the chicken into smallish pieces, removing the bones. Wash the lettuce, chicory (Belgian endive) and watercress. Tear them into bite size pieces and arrange them on a serving plate.

Toss each piece of pear and peach in lemon juice, to prevent browning. Arrange them, with the chicken and grapes on the plate. Top with a slice of lemon.

Blend together the cottage cheese, lemon juice, salt, pepper and paprika. Serve this sauce separately.

Coq à l'Orange

Metric/Imperial
1 × 1 kg/2 lb roasting chicken, cut into neat
    joints
15 g/½ oz butter
0.5 × 15 ml spoon/½ tablespoon corn oil
2 rashers bacon, rinded and chopped
4 small pickling onions
175 ml/6 fl oz fresh orange juice
150 ml/5 fl oz chicken stock
1 clove garlic, crushed (optional)
1 bouquet garni
salt
freshly ground black pepper
TO GARNISH:
finely chopped parsley
grated orange rind

American
1 × 2 lb roasting chicken, cut into
    neat joints
1 tablespoon butter
½ tablespoon corn oil
2 slices bacon, rinded and
    chopped
4 small pickling onions
¾ cup fresh orange juice
⅔ cup chicken bouillon
1 clove garlic, crushed (optional)
1 bouquet garni
salt
freshly ground black pepper
TO GARNISH:
finely chopped parsley
grated orange rind

Wipe the chicken pieces with a damp cloth.
Heat the butter and oil together in a flameproof
casserole. Add the chicken joints and cook them
quickly until browned all over. Remove the
chicken from the casserole.

In the same butter and oil fry the bacon and
onions until lightly browned. Return the chicken to
the casserole. Add the orange juice, stock
(bouillon), garlic, bouquet garni, salt and
pepper. Bring to the boil, cover and cook
gently in a preheated moderate oven
(160°C/325°F, Gas Mark 3) or simmer
gently on top of the stove for 1 hour.

Serve sprinkled with parsley
and orange rind.

Right: Spanish chicken

Spanish Chicken

Metric/Imperial
4 joints roasting chicken
salt
freshly ground black pepper
15 g/½ oz butter
0.5 × 15 ml spoon/½ tablespoon corn oil
2 large onions, sliced
2 cloves garlic, crushed (optional)
0.5 kg/1 lb tomatoes, skinned and chopped
300 ml/½ pint chicken stock
100 g/4 oz button mushrooms
chopped parsley to garnish

American
4 joints roasting chicken
salt
freshly ground black pepper
1 tablespoon butter
½ tablespoon corn oil
2 cups sliced onion
2 cloves garlic, crushed
    (optional)
2 cups skinned, chopped tomatoes
1¼ cups chicken bouillon
1 cup button mushrooms
chopped parsley to garnish

Wash and dry the chicken. Season it well with
salt and pepper. Heat the butter and oil in a frying
pan (skillet). Add the chicken joints and cook them
quickly until golden all over. Transfer them to a
casserole.

Fry the onions and garlic for 5 minutes, then
add the tomatoes and stock (bouillon). Bring to the
boil. Add the mushrooms and more seasoning if
required. Add this mixture to the chicken.

Cover the casserole and cook in a preheated
moderate oven (160°C/325°F, Gas Mark 3) for 1
hour. Serve sprinkled
with parsley.

Devilled Chicken Legs

Metric/Imperial

SAUCE:

1.5 × 15 ml spoons/1½ tablespoons vegetable oil

0.5 × 15 ml spoon/½ tablespoon Worcestershire
    sauce

0.5 × 15 ml spoon/½ tablespoon tarragon vinegar

0.5 × 15 ml spoon/½ tablespoon finely chopped
    onion

1 × 2.5 ml spoon/½ teaspoon French mustard

salt

freshly ground black pepper

4 chicken legs

225 g/8 oz mushrooms, peeled

parsley to garnish

American

SAUCE:

1½ tablespoons vegetable oil

½ tablespoon Worcestershire sauce

½ tablespoon tarragon vinegar

½ tablespoon finely chopped onion

½ teaspoon French mustard

salt

freshly ground black pepper

4 chicken legs

2 cups peeled mushrooms

parsley to garnish

Mix together the oil, Worcestershire sauce, vinegar, onion, mustard, salt and pepper. Score the chicken legs with the point of a sharp knife and brush them liberally with the sauce.

Place them in a grill pan (broiling pan) under a hot grill (broiler) for 8 to 10 minutes, basting frequently. Then turn the chicken legs over, brush them with more sauce and continue grilling (broiling) for a further 8 to 10 minutes, or until cooked.

Brush the mushrooms with any remaining sauce and add them to the grill pan (broiling pan) for the last 5 minutes of the cooking time.

Serve very hot, garnished with parsley.

Above: Devilled chicken legs

Roast Turkey

With smaller birds on the market now, turkeys no longer need to be reserved for the Christmas houseful of guests. Remember, too, that turkeys carry a considerable weight of bone, so allow at least 350 g/12 oz per person.

The greatest problem with a turkey is to keep it moist during its lengthy cooking time. A good rich stuffing will help, both inside the skin of the neck and right inside the bird, and you should cover the breast with fat or fat bacon. Frequent basting, too, is essential, unless the bird is wrapped in foil.

Add the weight of the stuffing to the weight of the bird before you calculate cooking times. Choose the *Quick Roasting Method* for prime birds; the *Slower Roasting Method* for frozen or poorer quality birds.

Always allow frozen poultry to thaw completely before cooking and remember that a large turkey could take up to 48 hours, at room temperature, to thaw.

Quick Roasting Method
Place the turkey in a preheated hot oven (220–230°C/425–450°F, Gas Mark 7–8). Reduce the temperature after 30 minutes, to 190–200°C/375–400°F, Gas Mark 5–6.

Cooking times
Turkeys up to 12 lb – 15 minutes per lb plus an extra 15 minutes
12 lb–21 lb – 27 minutes per lb plus an extra 27 minutes
21 lb and over – allow 10 minutes for each additional lb
If the bird is exceptionally broad breasted be a little generous with the cooking time.

Slower Roasting Method
Place the turkey in a preheated moderate oven (180–190°C/350–375°F, Gas Mark 4–5).

Cooking times
Turkeys up to 12 lb – 25 minutes per lb plus an extra 25 minutes
12 lb–21 lb – 47 minutes per lb plus an extra 47 minutes
21 lb and over – allow 10 minutes for each additional lb
If the bird is exceptionally broad breasted allow an extra 5 minutes per lb.

If you are using a covered roasting pan or foil, allow an extra 15–20 minutes, but not if using cooking film or roasting bags.

Thirty minutes before cooking is complete, remove the lid of the roasting pan, or open the foil, so that the skin may become crisp and brown.

Above: Roast turkey

Accompaniments
Boil the meat juices rapidly for a few minutes, to produce a rich but non-fattening gravy, and serve your roast turkey with braised celery, roast onions and a fresh tomato salad.

Turkey Leftovers
*Serve shredded cold roast turkey in a yogurt and herb dressing – natural yogurt, blended with chopped celery leaves, chopped chives, grated horseradish, lemon juice, paprika, parsley, salt and garlic.
*Mince cold cooked turkey together with some cold boiled or steamed leeks to make a Turkey and Leek Pâté.
*Shred cold roast turkey, boiled ham and roast beef, and serve them on a bed of spinach and watercress, with a well flavoured oil and vinegar dressing.
*Mince some cold roast turkey, season it well with herbs and minced onion. Moisten it with a little stock (bouillon) and use it as a stuffing for a joint of lamb or veal.

Boiled Ham
or Bacon Joints

Joints of ham or bacon should be soaked in cold water for at least 12 hours before cooking, then drain off the soaking water.

Stud the meat with cloves and place it in a very large saucepan together with sliced onions, carrots and celery.

Cover with plenty of fresh cold water, mixed with dry cider or fresh orange juice. Add a bouquet garni, some whole black peppercorns and slivers of orange peel.

Bring to the boil, reduce heat, cover and simmer gently, allowing 20 minutes per lb plus an extra 20 minutes for tender cuts; 35 minutes per lb plus an extra 35 minutes for less tender cuts. Add some sliced cooking (baking) apple just 10 to 15 minutes before cooking is complete.

Serve the ham hot, as it is; or, remove its skin and spread it with a mixture of prepared mustard and crumbled rolls, and bake in a hot oven until crisp. Or, allow the ham to cool in the liquid and serve it cold, thinly sliced with salad.

Gammon (Ham) Steaks
with Orange Sauce

Metric/Imperial
150 ml/¼ pint dry cider
150 ml/¼ pint orange juice
2 × 15 ml spoons/2 tablespoons low calorie
marmalade
4 gammon steaks
1 × 15 ml spoon/1 tablespoon caraway seeds
orange slices to garnish

American
⅔ cup dry hard cider
⅔ cup orange juice
2 tablespoons low calorie
marmalade
4 smoked ham slices
1 tablespoon caraway seeds
orange slices to garnish

Boil together the cider, orange juice and marmalade over a high flame until well reduced and slightly thickened.

Sprinkle the gammon (ham) steaks with caraway seeds and grill (broil) them for 5 minutes on each side.

Pour the orange sauce over the gammon (ham) steaks and garnish with orange slices before serving.

Pork Chops with Lemon
and Ginger

Metric/Imperial
2 × 15 ml spoons/2 tablespoons corn oil
grated rind of 2 lemons
4 × 15 ml spoons/4 tablespoons lemon juice
2 × 15 ml spoons/2 tablespoons clear honey
2 × 5 ml spoons/2 teaspoons ground ginger
salt
freshly ground black pepper
4 pork chops
TO GARNISH:
lemon
parsley

American
2 tablespoons corn oil
grated rind of 2 lemons
¼ cup of lemon juice
2 tablespoons clear honey
2 teaspoons ground ginger
salt
freshly ground black pepper
4 pork chops
TO GARNISH:
lemon
parsley

Mix together the oil, lemon rind, lemon juice, honey, ginger, salt and pepper. Place the chops in a single layer in a shallow dish. Pour the marinade over them and leave for at least 3 hours, turning the chops occasionally.

Drain the chops and grill (broil) them under a hot grill (broiler) for 15 minutes, turning once during cooking and basting with the marinade.

Garnish with lemon and parsley if wished.

Ham and Chicken Mould

Above: Ham and chicken mould

Metric/Imperial
1½ envelopes unflavoured gelatine
700 ml/1⅛ pint rich chicken stock
2 hard-boiled eggs
275 g/10 oz cooked chicken, diced
225 g/8 oz cooked lean ham, diced
few cooked peas
1 × 0.5 kg/1 lb can asparagus tips

American
1½ envelopes unflavored gelatin
2¾ cups rich chicken bouillon
2 hard-cooked eggs
1¼ cups diced cooked chicken
1 cup diced cooked lean ham
few cooked peas
1 × 1 lb can asparagus tips

Dissolve the gelatine in the stock (bouillon), according to the directions on the packet. Allow it to cool slightly.

Rinse out a 1.2 litre/2 pint (5 cup) mould with cold water. Pour a little gelatine into the mould and leave it to set.

Shell and slice the eggs and arrange them in a neat design on the aspic. Spoon a very little aspic over the egg and put it into the refrigerator until firmly set.

Cover with a layer of peas and neatly diced chicken and ham. Cover with more aspic and allow to set in the refrigerator again.

Continue like this, using the very well drained asparagus for the final layer. Cover with the remaining aspic and chill until firmly set.

Dip the mould in warm water for a few seconds, then invert it on to a serving dish. Serve with salad.

33

Chinese Kidneys

Metric/Imperial

4 lambs' kidneys, skinned, cored and sliced
2 × 15 ml spoons/2 tablespoons lemon juice
1 small cauliflower, broken into small florets
2 × 15 ml spoons/2 tablespoons corn oil
4 spring onions, cut into 2.5 cm/1 inch lengths
1 × 15 ml spoon/1 tablespoon soya sauce
2 × 15 ml spoons/2 tablespoons water
1 × 5 ml spoon/1 teaspoon salt

Soak the kidneys in lemon juice for 10 minutes. Drain them, reserving the juice.

Cook the cauliflower in boiling salted water for 3 minutes, then drain it well.

Heat the oil in a frying pan (skillet). Fry the drained kidneys, cauliflower and spring onions (scallions) for 2 minutes.

American

4 lamb kidneys, skinned, cored and sliced
2 tablespoons lemon juice
4 cups cauliflower florets
2 tablespoons corn oil
4 scallions, cut into 1 inch lengths
1 tablespoon soya sauce
2 tablespoons water
1 teaspoon salt

Mix together the soya sauce, water, salt and the lemon juice in which the kidneys soaked. Add this to the pan and cook gently for 3 minutes, stirring all the time. Serve immediately.

34

Liver and Leeks

Metric/Imperial
0.5 kg/1 lb lambs' liver
2 × 15 ml spoons/2 tablespoons lemon juice
2 × 15 ml spoons/2 tablespoons soya sauce
2 leeks, cut into 2.5 cm/1 inch pieces
1 × 15 ml spoon/1 tablespoon corn oil
2 spring onions, chopped
salt

American
1 lb lamb liver
2 tablespoons lemon juice
2 tablespoons soya sauce
1 cup leeks, cut into 1 inch pieces
1 tablespoon corn oil
2 scallions, chopped
salt

Wash the liver and cut it into strips, 5 cm × 1 cm/2 inch × 1 inch. Cover with boiling water for only 1 minute. Drain it well.

Mix together the lemon juice and soya sauce. Pour this over the liver and toss well.

Cook the leeks in boiling salted water for 4 to 5 minutes, then drain them well.

Heat the oil and fry the liver over a fierce heat for 1 minute, stirring all the time. Add the spring onions (scallions) and drained leeks and a pinch of salt. Heat quickly, stirring, for 1 minute. Serve immediately.

Liver and leeks

Above: Summer fish (page 44)

36

Fish and seafood

Filleting a Fish

1. Cut off the head. Remove and discard the intestines, saving any roe to use separately. Wash the fish well, inside and out, under cold running water.

2. Split the fish along the belly.

3. Open out the fish on a wooden surface, cut side downward, and run your fingers firmly along the backbone.

4. Turn the fish over again and you will find that the bones can be removed very easily. Wash again thoroughly, under cold running water, and dry with kitchen paper (paper towels).

Somerset Fish

Metric/Imperial
4 trout or herring
salt
freshly ground black pepper
3 small onions, peeled and cut into rings
2 eating apples, peeled and finely chopped
pinch of cinnamon
juice of 2 oranges
150 ml/¼ pint fish stock
2 bay leaves
orange slices to garnish

American
4 trout or herring
salt
freshly ground black pepper
3 small onions, peeled and cut
    into rings
1 cup finely chopped dessert
    apple
pinch of cinnamon
juice of 2 oranges
⅔ cup fish bouillon
2 bay leaves
orange slices to garnish

Wash and dry the fish and sprinkle them with salt and pepper. Put them in a casserole.

Add the onions, apples and cinnamon. Pour in the orange juice and fish stock (bouillon). Add the bay leaves.

Cook in a preheated moderately hot oven (190°C/375°F, Gas Mark 5) for 30 to 35 minutes.

Serve garnished with orange slices.

Somerset Fish could be served cold as part of a buffet, or as a summer supper dish. If you plan to serve it cold, cook it for only 25 to 30 minutes, then allow it to cool in the liquor. It will continue to cook slightly as it cools. Serve with a selection of fresh, crisp salads.

Steamed Trout with Mushrooms and Shrimps

Metric/Imperial
4 trout*
1 × 2.5 ml spoon/½ teaspoon salt
freshly ground black pepper
4 × 15 ml spoons/4 tablespoons lemon juice
sprigs of fresh dill
50–75 g/2–3 oz mushrooms, sliced
TO GARNISH:
few peeled prawns
lemon quarters

American
4 trout*
½ teaspoon salt
freshly ground black pepper
¼ cup lemon juice
sprigs of fresh dill
½ cup sliced mushrooms
TO GARNISH:
few shelled shrimp
lemon quarters

Clean the fish thoroughly. Place them on a large sheet of foil or greaseproof paper. Sprinkle them with salt, pepper, lemon juice and dill. Fold in the foil or paper, so that none of the juice can escape. Place it between two plates, and stand them on a pan of boiling water. Steam for 10 to 15 minutes, or until cooked. Transfer to a hot serving dish.

Strain the juice from the foil into a small pan. Bring it to the boil. Add the mushrooms and allow to simmer for 4 to 5 minutes.

Pour the mushrooms and juice over the fish, and garnish with prawns (shrimp) and lemon quarters.

*This same recipe could apply equally well to other fish, such as plaice (flounder), sole, haddock or cod.

Below: Somerset fish

38

Shrimp and Halibut Salad

Metric/Imperial

300 ml/½ pint water
2 × 15 ml spoons/2 tablespoons lemon juice
1 bay leaf
salt
freshly ground black pepper
175 g/6 oz halibut
225 g/8 oz peeled shrimp
1 small green pepper, deseeded with pith removed
    and diced
1 small red pepper, deseeded with pith removed
    and diced
few lettuce leaves, or
    sprigs of watercress

SAUCE:
1 × 2.5 ml spoon/½ teaspoon French mustard
2 × 15 ml spoons/2 tablespoons corn oil
1 × 15 ml spoon/1 tablespoon wine vinegar
2 hard boiled egg yolks, sieved
2 × 15 ml spoons/2 tablespoons soured cream
black olives to garnish

American

1¼ cups water
2 tablespoons lemon juice
1 bay leaf
salt
freshly ground black pepper
6 oz halibut
1 cup shelled shrimp
1 small green pepper, deseeded
    with pith removed and diced
1 small red pepper, deseeded with
    pith removed and diced
few lettuce leaves, or
    sprigs of watercress

SAUCE:
½ teaspoon French mustard
2 tablespoons corn oil
1 tablespoon wine vinegar
2 hard cooked egg yolks, strained
2 tablespoons sour cream
ripe olives to garnish

Bring to the boil, water, lemon juice, bay leaf, salt and pepper. Add the piece of halibut and poach it gently until barely cooked. Allow it to cool in the liquid.

When cold, cut it into small pieces and blend them with the shrimp. Add the green and red pepper. Arrange the fish and pepper on a bed of lettuce or watercress.

Whisk together the mustard, oil, wine vinegar, egg yolks, and soured cream. Season with salt and pepper.

Pour this sauce over the fish and pepper, and garnish with olives.

Lemony Fish

Metric/Imperial

0.75 kg/1½ lb cod, haddock or turbot
    fillets, or a combination of the three
1 × 2.5 ml spoon/½ teaspoon salt
freshly ground black pepper
6–8 coriander seeds, crushed
1 red pepper, deseeded with pith removed and
    finely chopped
1 green pepper, deseeded with pith removed and
    finely chopped
50 g/2 oz white grapes, peeled, halved and
    deseeded
juice of 1 lemon
300 ml/½ pint water

American

1½ lb cod, haddock or turbot
    fillets or a combination of the
    three
½ teaspoon salt
freshly ground black pepper
6–8 coriander seeds, crushed
½ cup finely chopped red pepper,
    deseeded with pith removed
½ cup finely chopped green
    pepper, deseeded with pith
    removed
½ cup peeled, halved and de-
    seeded white grapes
juice of 1 lemon
1¼ cups water

Arrange the fish in a single layer in a shallow casserole. Season it with salt, pepper and coriander.

Add the peppers, grapes, lemon juice and water. Cover the dish and bake in a preheated moderate oven (180°C/350°F, Gas Mark 4) for 20 to 30 minutes.

Above: Plaice (flounder) with mushroom
sauce in preparation.

Plaice (Flounder) with Mushroom Sauce

Metric/Imperial
0.75 kg/1½ lb plaice fillets
2 × 15 ml spoons/2 tablespoons lemon juice
salt
freshly ground pepper
15 g/½ oz butter
225 g/½ lb mushrooms, sliced
6 spring onions, sliced
1 egg, beaten

American
1½ lb flounder fillets
2 tablespoons lemon juice
salt
freshly ground black pepper
1 tablespoon butter
2 cups sliced mushrooms
6 scallions, sliced
1 egg, beaten

Sprinkle the plaice (flounder) fillets with lemon juice, salt and pepper and allow to stand for 15 minutes.

Heat the butter in a pan. Add the mushrooms and spring onions (scallions) and fry quickly for 4 to 5 minutes.

Transfer the vegetables to a casserole. Arrange the plaice (flounder) fillets on top.

Cover with foil and bake in a preheated moderately hot oven (190°C/375°F, Gas Mark 5) for 15 to 20 minutes.

Transfer the fish to a warm serving plate.

Liquidize (blend) the mushrooms, spring onions (scallions) and cooking liquor. Add a spoonful of this purée to the beaten egg, whisking all the time. Return this mixture to the rest of the mushroom purée. Reheat gently, without allowing to boil, and stirring all the time. Check the seasoning before serving this sauce with the fish.

A crisp green salad with a lemon dressing would go well with this dish.

Fisherman's Stew

Metric/Imperial

0.75–1 kg/1½–2 lb mixed fresh fish (try to
   include at least 5 varieties)
1 × 15 ml spoon/1 tablespoon corn oil
1 large onion, chopped
1 clove garlic, crushed
100 g/4 oz tomatoes, skinned, deseeded and
   chopped
bouquet garni
pinch of saffron
salt
freshly ground black pepper
pinch of nutmeg
600 ml/1 pint boiling water
2 × 15 ml spoons/2 tablespoons fresh orange juice
1 × 15 ml spoon/1 tablespoon grated orange rind

American

1½–2 lb mixed fresh fish (try to
   include at least 5 varieties)
1 tablespoon corn oil
1 cup chopped onion
1 clove garlic, crushed
½ cup skinned, deseeded and
   chopped tomatoes
bouquet garni
pinch of saffron
salt
freshly ground black pepper
pinch of nutmeg
2½ cups boiling water
2 tablespoons fresh orange juice
1 tablespoon grated orange rind

Clean all the fish, discarding any skin or bones.
Cut the fish into pieces of similar size. Separate
the softer, quicker cooking fish from the rest and
put it on one side.

Heat the oil in a large pan. Add the onion and
cook until soft, stirring constantly. Add the garlic,
tomatoes, bouquet garni, saffron, salt, pepper and
nutmeg.

Add the boiling water and the firm fleshed fish
and bring back to the boil. Cook rapidly,
uncovered, for 10 minutes.

Add the softer fish, orange juice and grated
orange rind. Continue cooking for a further 5
minutes, stirring from time to time. Serve very
hot.

Serve your chosen vegetables separately, after
the Fisherman's Stew – some plainly steamed leeks
with a sprinkling of lemon juice, or a peppery
turnip purée are suggested.

Curried Haddock Mousse

Metric/Imperial

0.5 kg/1 lb fresh or smoked haddock
0.5 × 15 ml spoon/½ tablespoon corn oil
1 medium onion, finely chopped
2 × 5 ml spoons/2 teaspoons curry powder
100 g/4 oz cottage cheese
5 cm/2 inch cucumber, finely chopped
2 × 15 ml spoons/2 tablespoons finely chopped
   parsley
1 × 15 ml spoon/1 tablespoon lemon juice
7.5 g/¼ oz gelatine
1 egg white

American

1 lb fresh or smoked haddock
½ tablespoon corn oil
½ cup finely chopped onion
2 teaspoons curry powder
½ cup cottage cheese
½ cup finely chopped cucumber
2 tablespoons finely chopped
   parsley
1 tablespoon lemon juice
1 envelope gelatin
1 egg white

Steam the haddock between two plates, over a
pan of boiling water, for 10 to 15 minutes. Leave it
to cool, then flake it with a fork, discarding any
skin or bones.

Brush a frying pan (skillet) with oil and fry the
onion and curry powder in this for 5 to 7 minutes.
Allow it to cool, then stir it into the cottage cheese.
Stir in the fish, cucumber and parsley.

Heat the lemon juice – a metal soup ladle held
over the gas flame is a useful utensil for this
operation. Dissolve the gelatine in the hot lemon
juice, then add it to the fish mixture, blending it in
thoroughly.

Whip the egg white until stiff and fold it into
the mixture. Transfer the mousse to a mould,
previously rinsed out with cold water, and leave in
the refrigerator to set. Invert on to a plate before
serving with a selection of carefully prepared
salads:
*cucumber and beetroot (beet) mixed with a little
soured cream;
*peeled and thinly sliced tomatoes, topped with
plenty of black pepper, a few onion rings and a
spoonful of fresh orange juice;
*a mixed green salad of lettuce, chicory, spinach
and watercress in an oil and vinegar dressing;
*cold cooked French beans and leeks, well
seasoned and tossed in an oil and lemon dressing.

This mousse would make a perfect first course,
prepared in individual cocotte dishes.

Soused Herrings

Metric/Imperial
4 herrings
1 onion, sliced
wine vinegar
water
3 bay leaves
2 cloves
12 allspice
2 blades of mace
1 × 5 ml spoon/1 teaspoon salt

American
4 herrings
1 cup sliced onion
wine vinegar
water
3 bay leaves
2 cloves
12 allspice
2 blades of mace
1 teaspoon salt

Clean the herrings, and remove the backbones, following the illustrated instructions at the beginning of this chapter.

Lay the herrings, skin side down, on a working surface and place some onion slices on each. Roll them up, from head to tail and secure them with toothpicks.

Place them in a casserole. Add enough vinegar and water to cover the fish, in the proportion of 3 parts vinegar to 1 part water. Add the bay leaves, cloves, allspice, mace and salt. Cover and cook in a preheated cool oven (150°C/300°F, Gas Mark 2) for 3 hours, or until the fish is cooked. The liquid must not be allowed to boil.

Transfer the fish to a serving dish and strain the liquor over them. Allow to cool, then chill in the refrigerator.

Leftover Fish

*Mix flaked cooked fish with sprigs of lightly steamed cauliflower, a few olives, slivers of green pepper (deseeded with pith removed) and toss in French dressing.
*Cover a layer of flaked cooked fish with a well seasoned spinach purée, top with a little grated Edam cheese and grill lightly.
*Mash to a purée some flaked cooked fish, anchovy essence, lemon juice, salt and pepper, and use this mixture to stuff hard boiled (hard cooked) eggs or tomatoes.

Thon à la Provençale

Metric/Imperial
2 × 200 g/7 oz cans tuna
juice of ½ lemon
salt
freshly ground black pepper
4 anchovy fillets
0.5 × 15 ml spoon/½ tablespoon corn oil
1 large onion, chopped
1 clove garlic, crushed
175 g/6 oz tomatoes, skinned, deseeded and
  chopped
bouquet garni
150 ml/¼ pint fish stock, or
  120 ml/4 fl oz water and
  2 × 15 ml spoons/2 tablespoons lemon juice
finely chopped parsley to garnish

American
2 × 7 oz cans tuna
juice of ½ lemon
salt
freshly ground black pepper
4 anchovy fillets
½ tablespoon corn oil
1 cup chopped onion
1 clove garlic, crushed
¾ cup skinned, deseeded and
  chopped tomatoes
bouquet garni
⅔ cup fish stock, or
  ½ cup water and
  2 tablespoons lemon juice
finely chopped parsley to garnish

Remove the tuna from the cans very carefully, so that they stay in shape. Arrange them side by side in an ovenproof serving dish. Sprinkle them with lemon juice and season lightly with salt and pepper. Arrange the anchovy fillets on top.

Brush a frying pan (skillet) with oil. Heat it and fry the onion and garlic until softened. Add the tomatoes, bouquet garni and fish stock (bouillon), or water and lemon juice. Bring to the boil and cook rapidly, uncovered, until reduced and thickened.

Pour the sauce over the tuna, cover and bake in a preheated moderate oven (180°C/350°F, Gas Mark 4) for 10 to 15 minutes. Discard the bouquet garni. Serve sprinkled with parsley.

Right: Soused herrings

Sea Scallops with Peppers

Metric/Imperial

0.5 kg/1 lb scallops
2 spring onions, finely chopped
0.5 × 15 ml spoon/½ tablespoon corn oil
1 × 5 ml spoon/1 teaspoon salt
2 green peppers, deseeded with pith removed and
  sliced
4 × 15 ml spoons/4 tablespoons water

American

1 lb sea scallops
2 scallions, finely chopped
½ tablespoon corn oil
1 teaspoon salt
2 cups sliced green pepper,
  deseeded with pith removed
¼ cup water

Wash, trim and slice the scallops. Brush a frying pan (skillet) with oil. Heat it and fry the scallops and spring onions (scallions) in this for 3 minutes, stirring all the time. Add the salt and mix well.

Add the peppers and the water and bring to the boil stirring all the time. Simmer for 2 minutes, then serve immediately.

Summer Fish

Metric/Imperial

4 mackerel, herring or mullet
600 ml/1 pint dry cider or fish stock
750 ml/1¼ pints water
juice of 1 lemon
2 onions, sliced
1 × 5 ml spoon/1 teaspoon dill seeds
peel of ½ lemon
8 whole black peppercorns
2 bay leaves
1 × 2.5 ml spoon/½ teaspoon salt
French mustard
chopped parsley to garnish

American

4 mackerel, herring or mullet
2½ cups dry hard cider or fish bouillon
3 cups water
juice of 1 lemon
1 cup sliced onion
1 teaspoon dill seeds
peel of ½ lemon
8 whole black peppercorns
2 bay leaves
½ teaspoon salt
French mustard
chopped parsley to garnish

Clean the fish, removing the fins and tails. Put the cider, water, lemon juice, onion, dill seeds, lemon peel, peppercorns, bay leaves and salt

Below: Sea scallops with peppers

in a saucepan. Bring to the boil and allow to simmer for 10 minutes. Strain this liquid and leave it to cool.

Arrange the fish in a wide pan. Cover them with the cooled liquid. Bring to the boil and simmer very gently for 10 minutes, or until the fish are no longer pink inside.

Carefully lift the fish out of the liquid. Divide each fish into two fillets, discarding all the skin and bones. Arrange the fish fillets on a serving plate.

Strain off 900 ml/1½ pints (3¾ cups) of the liquid. Stir in a little French mustard to taste. Pour this over the fish. Chill before serving sprinkled with chopped parsley.

Summer Fish with Orange

Metric/Imperial
4 large fillets of sole, plaice or whiting
salt
freshly ground black pepper
1 × 15 ml spoon/1 tablespoon orange juice
1 × 15 ml spoon/1 tablespoon grated orange rind
4 thick slices orange, peeled
SAUCE:
100 g/4 oz cottage cheese
2 hard boiled egg yolks, sieved
2 × 15 ml spoons/2 tablespoons grated orange rind
salt
freshly ground black pepper
TO GARNISH:
paprika
white grapes, skinned, halved and seeded

American
4 large fillets of sole, flounder or whiting
salt
freshly ground black pepper
1 tablespoon orange juice
1 tablespoon grated orange rind
4 thick slices orange, peeled
SAUCE:
½ cup cottage cheese
2 hard cooked egg yolks, strained
2 tablespoons grated orange rind
salt
freshly ground black pepper
TO GARNISH:
paprika
white grapes, skinned, halved and seeded

Season the fillets lightly with salt, pepper, orange juice and orange rind. Roll them up, from head to tail, and secure them with a toothpick.

Steam them gently between two plates over a pan of boiling water until they are just cooked, but not in danger of collapse. They will continue to cook a little more as they cool.

When quite cold, carefully transfer each fish fillet to a slice of orange. Arrange on serving dish.

Rub the cottage cheese through a sieve (strainer). Blend in the egg yolks, salt, pepper and orange peel. Spoon a little sauce over each fillet, sprinkle with paprika and garnish with grapes.

Chinese Braised Fish

Metric/Imperial
1 × 1 kg/2 lb whole fish (bream, bass or snapper are most suitable)
1 × 5 ml spoon/1 teaspoon salt
4 Chinese dried mushrooms
1 × 5 ml spoon/1 teaspoon corn oil
4 spring onions, cut into 1 cm/½ inch lengths
6 water chestnuts, sliced
1 × 5 ml spoon/1 teaspoon fresh ginger, finely chopped
2 cloves garlic, crushed
300 ml/½ pint fish stock or water
2 × 15 ml spoons/2 tablespoons soya sauce
1 × 15 ml spoon/1 tablespoon lemon juice

American
1 × 2 lb whole fish (bream, bass or snapper are most suitable)
1 teaspoon salt
4 Chinese dried mushrooms
1 teaspoon corn oil
4 scallions, cut into ½ inch lengths
6 water chestnuts, sliced
1 teaspoon fresh ginger, finely chopped
2 cloves garlic, crushed
1¼ cups fish bouillon or water
2 tablespoons soya sauce
1 tablespoon lemon juice

Clean the fish, leaving on the head and tail. Wipe it inside and out with paper towels. Make two gashes on each side, in the thickest part, with a sharp knife. Sprinkle the fish well with salt.

Soak the mushrooms in warm water for 20 minutes, rinse them, squeeze them dry and remove their stalks, which may be used for flavouring soup. Cut the mushrooms into strips.

Heat the oil in a frying pan (skillet) large enough to take the whole fish. Fry the fish quickly on both sides until golden. Add the mushrooms, spring onions (scallions), water chestnuts, ginger, garlic, stock (bouillon), soya sauce and lemon juice. Cover the pan, bring to the boil and simmer for about 30 minutes, carefully turning the fish once.

Serve on a large heated plate with the sauce poured over.

Above: Chinese braised fish

Vegetables

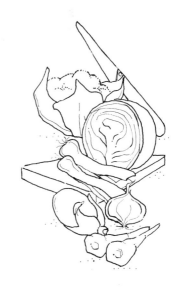

Stuffed Aubergines (Eggplants)

Metric/Imperial
3 large aubergines
1 large onion, chopped
100 g/4 oz tomatoes, peeled, deseeded and
  chopped
2 × 15 ml spoons/2 tablespoons chopped parsley
50 g/2 oz mushrooms, chopped
1 × 5 ml spoon/1 teaspoon oregano
salt
freshly ground black pepper

American
3 large eggplants
1 cup chopped onion
½ cup peeled, deseeded and
  chopped tomatoes
2 tablespoons chopped parsley
½ cup chopped mushrooms
1 teaspoon oregano
salt
freshly ground black pepper

Cut the aubergines (eggplants) in half lengthwise. Scoop out some of the flesh and chop it finely.

Boil the onion in very little salted water for 3 to 4 minutes, then drain it well.

Add it to the chopped aubergine (eggplant) flesh, together with the tomatoes, parsley, mushrooms, oregano, salt and pepper. Mix well and fill each aubergine (eggplant) half with this mixture. Brush the top of each with oil and bake in a preheated moderate oven (180°C/350°F, Gas Mark 4) for ¾ to 1 hour.

Serve hot or cold.

Stuffed Tomatoes

Metric/Imperial
4 large tomatoes
350 g/12 oz fresh spinach
salt
freshly ground black pepper
freshly grated nutmeg
1 clove garlic, crushed
2 × 15 ml spoons/2 tablespoons cottage cheese

American
4 large tomatoes
¾ lb fresh spinach
salt
freshly ground black pepper
freshly grated nutmeg
1 clove garlic, crushed
2 tablespoons cottage cheese

Cut the tops off the tomatoes and carefully scoop out the pulp, taking care not to damage the skins. Use the pulp for soups.

Wash the spinach thoroughly and cook it, without adding any more water, for 7 to 10 minutes in a tightly covered pan. Empty it into a sturdy metal colander and chop it finely, pressing out all the liquid. Season the spinach with salt, pepper and nutmeg. Blend in the garlic and cottage cheese.

Spoon the spinach mixture into the hollowed tomatoes and cook in a preheated moderate oven (180°C/350°F, Gas Mark 4) for 20 to 30 minutes. The tomatoes should be hot but not too soft.

Purée of Swedes

Metric/Imperial
1 kg/2 lb swedes
salt
freshly ground black pepper
pinch of ground ginger
4 × 15 ml spoons/4 tablespoons soured cream
chopped parsley to garnish

American
2 lb rutabaga
salt
freshly ground black pepper
pinch of ground ginger
4 tablespoons sour cream
chopped parsley to garnish

Peel the swedes (rutabaga) and cut them into even sized pieces. Boil them in salted water until they are soft enough to be rubbed through a sieve.

Season the swede (rutabaga) purée with more salt, pepper and ginger. Blend in the soured cream and reheat gently, without allowing it to boil.

Serve sprinkled with parsley.

Stuffed Cabbage Leaves

Metric/Imperial
4 large cabbage leaves
salt
1 × 15 ml spoon/1 tablespoon corn oil
1 onion, chopped
1 carrot, chopped
225 g/8 oz tomatoes, peeled, deseeded and chopped
100 g/4 oz mushrooms, chopped
freshly ground black pepper
freshly grated nutmeg
2 × 15 ml spoons/2 tablespoons finely chopped parsley
2 × 15 ml spoons/2 tablespoons beef stock

American
4 large cabbage leaves
salt
1 tablespoon corn oil
½ cup chopped onion
⅓ cup chopped carrot
1 cup peeled, deseeded and chopped tomatoes
1 cup chopped mushrooms
freshly ground black pepper
freshly grated nutmeg
2 tablespoons finely chopped parsley
2 tablespoons beef bouillon

Cook the cabbage leaves in a large pan of boiling salted water for 3 to 5 minutes. Drain and cool them. Spread each one out carefully and remove the hard stem from the base.

Heat half of the oil in a frying pan (skillet) and fry the onion and carrot for 5 minutes, stirring all the time. Add the tomatoes, mushrooms, salt, pepper, nutmeg and parsley. Allow to cook until the juice from the tomatoes has evaporated.

Let this mixture cool slightly, then divide it between the cabbage leaves. Fold the sides over, to trap the filling, and roll up the leaves carefully and neatly.

Brush a casserole with the remaining oil, and arrange the stuffed cabbage leaves in it, in a single layer.

Bake in a preheated moderate oven (180°C/350°F, Gas Mark 4) for 45 to 50 minutes, basting with a little stock (bouillon) from time to time. Serve hot.

Above: Stuffed cabbage leaves

Ratatouille

Metric/Imperial

1 medium aubergine, diced
225 g/8 oz courgettes, sliced
salt
1 × 15 ml spoon/1 tablespoon corn oil
4 medium onions, sliced
0.5 kg/1 lb tomatoes, skinned, deseeded and
  chopped
2 cloves garlic, chopped
1 green pepper, deseeded with pith removed and
  sliced
1 red pepper, deseeded with pith removed and
  sliced
freshly ground black pepper
chopped parsley to garnish

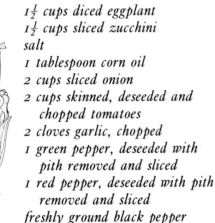

American

1½ cups diced eggplant
1½ cups sliced zucchini
salt
1 tablespoon corn oil
2 cups sliced onion
2 cups skinned, deseeded and
  chopped tomatoes
2 cloves garlic, chopped
1 green pepper, deseeded with
  pith removed and sliced
1 red pepper, deseeded with pith
  removed and sliced
freshly ground black pepper
chopped parsley to garnish

Place the aubergine (eggplant) and courgettes (zucchini) in a colander. Sprinkle them with salt and allow to stand for 30 minutes.

Heat the oil in a large pan. Add the onions, tomatoes and garlic and cook gently until the juice starts to flow from the tomatoes.

Add the green and red peppers, aubergines (eggplant) and courgettes (zucchini), salt and pepper. Stir well and cover with a tightly fitting lid. Simmer gently until the vegetables are cooked but still quite firm.

Serve hot or cold, sprinkled with parsley.

Mushrooms and Tomatoes

Metric/Imperial

1 × 15 ml spoon/1 tablespoon corn oil
15 g/½ oz butter
1 large onion, sliced
350 g/12 oz mushrooms, sliced
225 g/8 oz tomatoes, skinned, deseeded and chopped
salt
freshly ground black pepper
2 × 15 ml spoons/2 tablespoons finely chopped
  parsley

American

1 tablespoon corn oil
1 tablespoon butter
1 cup sliced onion
3 cups sliced mushrooms
1 cup skinned, deseeded and
  chopped tomatoes
salt
freshly ground black pepper
2 tablespoons finely chopped parsley

Heat together the oil and the butter in a thick pan. When hot add the onion and allow it to cook gently until soft and golden. Add the mushrooms and cook for a further 5 minutes.

Add the tomatoes, salt, pepper and parsley. Stir well, cover the pan and allow to simmer gently for 8 to 10 minutes.

Serve hot or cold.

Fenouil à la Grecque

Metric/Imperial

2 × 15 ml spoons/2 tablespoons corn oil
2 × 15 ml spoons/2 tablespoons water
2 tomatoes, skinned and chopped
6 coriander seeds
1 bay leaf
sprig of thyme
salt
freshly ground black pepper
3 or 4 fennel bulbs
juice of ½ lemon
finely chopped parsley to garnish

American

2 tablespoons corn oil
2 tablespoons water
⅓ cup skinned and chopped tomatoes
6 coriander seeds
1 bay leaf
sprig of thyme
salt
freshly ground black pepper
3 or 4 fennel bulbs
juice of ½ lemon
finely chopped parsley to garnish

In a saucepan put the oil, water, tomatoes, coriander seeds, bay leaf, thyme, salt and pepper.

Bring to the boil and simmer for 3 to 4 minutes.

Cut each fennel bulb into 4 pieces. Toss them in lemon juice. Add the fennel and lemon juice to the pan and cook gently until the fennel is tender but not too soft.

Using a slotted spoon transfer the fennel to a serving dish.

Cook the sauce quickly over a high flame until it starts to thicken. Pour this over the fennel and allow to cool. Garnish with parsley.

Above: Fenouil à la Grecque

Leeks with Tomato Sauce

Metric/Imperial

1 kg/2 lb leeks, washed and trimmed

SAUCE:

225 g/8 oz tomatoes, skinned, deseeded and
   chopped

1 × 15 ml spoon/1 tablespoon fresh orange juice

salt

freshly ground black pepper

finely chopped basil or oregano

American

2 lb leeks, washed and trimmed

SAUCE:

1 cup skinned, deseeded and
   chopped tomatoes

1 tablespoon fresh orange juice

salt

freshly ground black pepper

finely chopped basil or oregano

Steam the leeks in a double boiler or fish kettle until they are tender but not too soft.

Put the tomatoes, orange juice, salt, pepper and basil or oregano in a thick pan. Bring to the boil and allow to cook quite quickly until of the required consistency.

Pour this sauce over the leeks and serve hot.

French Beans with Garlic and Herbs

Metric/Imperial

0.5 kg/1 lb French beans, topped and tailed

salt

1 × 15 ml spoon/1 tablespoon corn oil

1 clove garlic, crushed

2 × 15 ml spoons/2 tablespoons finely chopped
   parsley

2 × 15 ml spoons/2 tablespoons finely chopped
   chives

pinch of cinnamon

freshly ground black pepper

American

1 lb French beans, cleaned

salt

1 tablespoon corn oil

1 clove garlic, crushed

2 tablespoons finely chopped
   parsley

2 tablespoons finely chopped
   chives

pinch of cinnamon

freshly ground black pepper

Steam the beans, or boil them gently in salted water until almost cooked but still slightly crisp.

Heat the oil in a thick pan. Add the garlic and stir it, over the heat, for 1 minute, then add the parsley, chives and cinnamon. Stir over the heat for a further minute, then add the drained beans.

Reheat gently, stirring to mix the beans, garlic and herbs thoroughly. Sprinkle with pepper before serving.

Danish Red Cabbage

Metric/Imperial

1 × 15 ml spoon/1 tablespoon corn oil

1 medium red cabbage, finely shredded

1 large onion, finely sliced

1 large cooking apple, finely sliced

1 × 15 ml spoon/1 tablespoon caraway seeds

2 × 15 ml spoons/2 tablespoons wine vinegar

pinch of soft brown sugar

salt

freshly ground black pepper

2 × 15 ml spoons/2 tablespoons beef stock

parsley to garnish

American

1 tablespoon corn oil

6 cups finely shredded red
   cabbage

1 cup finely sliced onion

1 cup finely sliced baking apple

1 tablespoon caraway seeds

2 tablespoons wine vinegar

pinch of light brown sugar

salt

freshly ground black pepper

2 tablespoons beef bouillon

parsley to garnish

Heat the oil in a large pan. Add the cabbage, onion, apple, caraway seeds, vinegar, sugar, salt, pepper and stock (bouillon). Stir well and cover with a close fitting lid.

Allow to cook gently for 40 to 45 minutes, stirring or shaking from time to time. Garnish with parsley.

Vegetable Tips

No vegetable *improves* while it is sitting in the rack in your kitchen. So it makes sense to buy vegetables as and when you need them.

Occasionally try serving your vegetables as a separate course, after the meat or fish, and enjoy the single flavour with no competition. Use leftover cooked vegetables in soups, or blend them – preferably while still warm – in a herby oil and vinegar dressing. Even unexpected vegetables like parsnips, peas or onions make good cooked salads.

Above: Danish red cabbage

Above: Cabbage with sweet and sour sauce

Braised Celery

Metric/Imperial
2 heads celery
15 g/½ oz butter
250 ml/¼ pint beef stock
1 × 2.5 ml spoon/½ teaspoon Worcestershire sauce
salt
freshly ground black pepper
finely chopped parsley to garnish

American
2 heads celery
1 tablespoon butter
1 cup beef bouillon
½ teaspoon Worcestershire sauce
salt
freshly ground black pepper
finely chopped parsley to garnish

Trim the celery and cut each head into quarters lengthwise. Any leaves or trimmings should be used to flavour soups or casseroles. Wash the celery well and dry it with paper towels.

Heat the butter in a large frying pan (skillet). Add the celery and toss it in the butter over a gentle heat until lightly browned all over. Add the stock (bouillon), Worcestershire sauce, salt and pepper. Cover with a lid or plate and cook for 10 to 15 minutes, or until the celery is tender but still crisp.

Serve sprinkled with parsley.

Cauliflower with Tomato Sauce

Metric/Imperial
SAUCE:
225 g/8 oz tomatoes, skinned, deseeded and
  chopped
salt
juice of ½ orange
1 × 2.5 ml spoon/½ teaspoon yeast extract
freshly ground black pepper

1 cauliflower, divided into sprigs
chopped parsley to garnish

American
SAUCE:
1 cup skinned, deseeded and
  chopped tomatoes
salt
juice of ½ orange
½ teaspoon yeast extract
freshly ground black pepper

1 cauliflower, divided into sprigs
chopped parsley to garnish

Put the tomatoes and salt in a pan and cook gently until the juice begins to flow. Add the orange juice, yeast extract and pepper and continue to cook until the tomatoes are soft enough to be sieved (strained). Sieve (strain) them, check the seasoning and keep this sauce warm.

Either steam the cauliflower, or boil it gently in salted water until tender but not too soft. Drain it well.

Pour the hot sauce over the cauliflower and sprinkle with parsley.

Cabbage with Sweet and Sour Sauce

Metric/Imperial
SAUCE:
1 × 15 ml spoon/1 tablespoon corn oil
1 large carrot, cut into thin strips
3 tomatoes, skinned, deseeded and chopped
150 ml/¼ pint beef stock
2 × 15 ml spoons/2 tablespoons soya sauce
1 × 5 ml spoon/1 teaspoon salt
1 × 15 ml spoon/1 tablespoon demerara sugar
2 × 15 ml spoons/2 tablespoons wine vinegar
1 × 300 g/11 oz can crushed pineapple

1 Chinese cabbage, or
  1 hard white cabbage

American
SAUCE:
1 tablespoon corn oil
1 large carrot, cut into thin
  strips
½ cup skinned, deseeded and
  chopped tomatoes
⅔ cup beef bouillon
2 tablespoons soya sauce
1 teaspoon salt
1 tablespoon brown sugar
2 tablespoons wine vinegar
1 × 11 oz can crushed pineapple

1 head Chinese cabbage, or
  1 head hard white cabbage

Heat the oil in a thick pan. Add the carrots and tomatoes and fry for 2 to 3 minutes, stirring all the time.

Add the stock (bouillon), soya sauce, salt, sugar, vinegar and pineapple. Bring to the boil and allow to simmer gently for 5 minutes.

Boil the cabbage in salted water for only 3 to 4 minutes. Drain it well, transfer it to a hot vegetable dish and top it with the sauce.

Salads

Salade Niçoise

Metric/Imperial

1 small lettuce, washed and cut into 8 wedges
2 hard-boiled eggs, sliced
2 small tomatoes, quartered
8 anchovy fillets
8 black olives
8 capers
½ red or green pepper, deseeded with pith removed and sliced

DRESSING:

3 × 15 ml spoons/3 tablespoons corn oil
1 × 15 ml spoon/1 tablespoon tarragon vinegar
2 cloves garlic, crushed
salt
freshly ground black pepper

2 × 15 ml spoons/2 tablespoons chopped fresh basil to garnish

American

1 small lettuce, washed and cut into 8 wedges
2 hard-cooked eggs, sliced
2 small tomatoes, quartered
8 anchovy fillets
8 ripe olives
8 capers
½ red or green pepper, deseeded with pith removed and sliced

DRESSING:

3 tablespoons corn oil
1 tablespoon tarragon vinegar
2 cloves garlic, crushed
salt
freshly ground black pepper

2 tablespoons chopped fresh basil to garnish

Arrange the lettuce, eggs, tomatoes, anchovies, olives, capers and pepper in a large salad bowl and chill while preparing the dressing.

Whisk together the oil, vinegar, garlic, salt and pepper, or shake them in a screw top jar.

Pour the well blended dressing over the chilled salad and sprinkle with basil before serving.

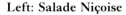

Left: Salade Niçoise

Raw Mushrooms with Lemon Dressing

Metric/Imperial

1 clove garlic

DRESSING:

1 × 2.5 ml spoon/½ teaspoon finely grated lemon peel
2 × 15 ml spoons/2 tablespoons corn oil
2 × 15 ml spoons/2 tablespoons lemon juice
pinch of grated nutmeg
salt
freshly ground black pepper
350 g/12 oz button mushrooms, sliced
finely chopped parsley to garnish

American

1 clove garlic

DRESSING:

½ teaspoon finely grated lemon peel
2 tablespoons corn oil
2 tablespoons lemon juice
pinch of grated nutmeg
salt
freshly ground black pepper
3 cups sliced button mushrooms
finely chopped parsley to garnish

Cut the garlic in half and rub the cut surface round the inside of your chosen salad bowl to give just a suspicion of the flavour without drowning the delicate taste of the raw mushrooms. The garlic may then be used for some other purpose.

In the bowl mix together the lemon peel, oil, lemon juice, nutmeg, salt and pepper. When well blended, toss the mushrooms in this until each slice glistens with dressing.

Cover and leave to stand at room temperature for 15 minutes. Sprinkle with parsley.

American Salad

Metric/Imperial

100 g/4 oz cooked French beans, sliced
100 g/4 oz raw mushrooms, sliced
50 g/2 oz cooked or canned sweetcorn
2 large tomatoes, skinned and sliced
½ red or green pepper, deseeded with pith removed and sliced
1 small onion, cut into rings

DRESSING:

3 × 15 ml spoons/3 tablespoons corn oil
1 × 15 ml spoon/1 tablespoon cider vinegar
salt
freshly ground black pepper
1 × 2.5 ml spoon/½ teaspoon dry mustard
black olives to garnish

American

½ cup sliced cooked French beans
1 cup sliced raw mushrooms
¼ cup cooked or canned corn kernels
¾ cup skinned and sliced tomato
½ red or green pepper, deseeded with pith removed and sliced
1 small onion, cut into rings

DRESSING:

3 tablespoons corn oil
1 tablespoon hard cider vinegar
salt
freshly ground black pepper
½ teaspoon dry mustard
ripe olives to garnish

Arrange the French beans, mushrooms, corn, tomatoes, pepper and onion in a salad bowl.

Whisk together the oil, vinegar, salt, pepper and mustard, or shake them together in a screw top jar.

Pour this dressing over the vegetables, toss well and garnish with olives.

Pepper and Olive Salad

Metric/Imperial

2 red peppers, cut into thin rings
2 green peppers, cut into thin rings
25 g/1 oz green olives, stoned
25 g/1 oz black olives, stoned

DRESSING:

3 × 15 ml spoons/3 tablespoons corn oil
1 × 15 ml spoon/1 tablespoon vinegar
salt
freshly ground black pepper

American

2 red peppers, cut into thin rings
2 green peppers, cut into thin rings
¼ cup pitted green olives
¼ cup pitted ripe olives

DRESSING:

3 tablespoons corn oil
1 tablespoon vinegar
salt
freshly ground black pepper

Put the peppers in a heatproof bowl, pour boiling water over them and allow to stand for 2 minutes. Rinse them well under cold running water, and discard any seeds.

Mix together the olives and peppers.

Whisk together the oil, vinegar, salt and pepper. Pour this over the peppers and olives and toss well before serving.

Italian Cauliflower Salad

Metric/Imperial

1 medium cauliflower, divided into sprigs
salt

DRESSING:

1 small onion, grated
3 × 15 ml spoons/3 tablespoons corn oil
1 × 15 ml spoon/1 tablespoon wine vinegar
0.5 × 15 ml spoon/½ tablespoon lemon juice
salt
freshly ground black pepper

TO GARNISH:

anchovy fillets, cut into small pieces
black olives, halved and stoned

American

1 medium cauliflower, divided
   into sprigs
salt

DRESSING:

¼ cup grated onion
3 tablespoons corn oil
1 tablespoon wine vinegar
½ tablesoon lemon juice
salt
freshly ground black pepper

TO GARNISH:

anchovy fillets, cut into small pieces
ripe olives, halved and pitted

Wash the cauliflower sprigs well, then either boil them gently in salted water, or steam them until they are still slightly crisp. Drain them well.

In a salad bowl mix together the onion, oil, wine vinegar, lemon juice, salt and pepper. Add the warm cauliflower sprigs and toss well.

Allow to cool, then chill well before serving garnished with olives and anchovy fillets.

61

Tomato Salad

Metric/Imperial

0.5 kg/1 lb tomatoes, peeled and sliced
3 × 15 ml spoons/3 tablespoons fresh orange juice
1 × 2.5 ml spoon/½ teaspoon salt
freshly ground black pepper
1 × 5 ml spoon/1 teaspoon finely chopped parsley
1 × 15 ml spoon/1 tablespoon chopped onion
  (optional)

American

2 cups peeled and sliced tomatoes
3 tablespoons fresh orange juice
½ teaspoon salt
freshly ground black pepper
1 teaspoon finely chopped parsley
1 tablespoon chopped onion
  (optional)

Arrange the tomatoes in a shallow serving dish. Sprinkle them with the orange juice, salt, pepper, parsley and onion (if liked).

Chill for at least 15 minutes before serving.

Cucumber Salad with Yogurt

Metric/Imperial

1 cucumber, peeled and very thinly sliced
2 × 5 ml spoons/2 teaspoons salt
1 clove garlic, crushed
1 × 15 ml spoon/1 tablespoon wine vinegar
120 ml/4 fl oz natural yogurt
1 × 15 ml spoon/1 tablespoon corn oil
1 × 15 ml spoon/1 tablespoon chopped dill, chives
  or parsley

American

1 cucumber, peeled and very
  thinly sliced
2 teaspoons salt
1 clove garlic, crushed
1 tablespoon wine vinegar
½ cup unflavored yogurt
1 tablespoon corn oil
1 tablespoon chopped dill, chives
  or parsley

Put the cucumber in a colander. Sprinkle it with half of the salt, cover with a saucer then a heavy weight, and allow it to drain for 1 hour.

Blend together the garlic and vinegar. Add the remaining salt and mix to a smooth paste. Stir this into the yogurt. Blend in the oil, dill, chives or parsley.

Pour this yogurt dressing over the well drained cucumber. Toss well and chill before serving.

Greek Salata

Metric/Imperial

¼ small red cabbage, shredded
100 g/4 oz pickled beetroot, cut into strips
50 g/2 oz cooked sliced French beans
1 × 15 ml spoon/1 tablespoon chopped oregano or
  marjoram
salt
freshly ground black pepper
DRESSING:
3 × 15 ml spoons/3 tablespoons corn oil
1 × 15 ml spoon/1 tablespoon wine vinegar
1 × 5 ml spoon/1 teaspoon coriander seeds,
  crushed
salt
freshly ground black pepper
TO GARNISH:
4 black olives, stoned and chopped
1 × 15 ml spoon/1 tablespoon capers

American

1½ cups shredded red cabbage
⅔ cup thinly sliced pickled beet
¼ cup sliced cooked French beans
1 tablespoon chopped oregano or
  marjoram
salt
freshly ground black pepper
DRESSING:
3 tablespoons corn oil
1 tablespoon wine vinegar
1 teaspoon coriander seeds,
  crushed
salt
freshly ground black pepper
TO GARNISH:
4 ripe olives, pitted and chopped
1 tablespoon capers

Mix together the red cabbage, beetroot (beet), French beans and oregano or marjoram in a salad bowl. Season with salt and pepper.

Whisk together the oil, wine vinegar, coriander, salt and pepper, or shake them in a screw top jar. Pour this dressing over the vegetables and toss well.

Garnish with olives and capers, and chill the salad for 30 minutes before serving.

Right: Tomato salad

Above: Salad quartet

Orange and Watercress Salad

Metric/Imperial

2 bunches watercress
2 large oranges, peeled

DRESSING:

0.5 × 2.5 ml spoon/¼ teaspoon salt
freshly ground black pepper
3 × 15 ml spoons/3 tablespoons corn oil
1 × 15 ml spoon/1 tablespoon wine vinegar

Wash the watercress, drain it well and tear it into bite size sprigs.

Cut the oranges into thin rounds. Mix them with the watercress in a salad bowl.

Whisk together the salt, pepper, oil and vinegar,

American

2 bunches watercress
2 large oranges, peeled

DRESSING:

¼ teaspoon salt
freshly ground black pepper
3 tablespoons corn oil
1 tablespoon wine vinegar

or shake them together in a screw top jar.

Pour this dressing over the watercress and oranges, and toss well before serving.

This salad is perfect with roast meat, poultry or game.

64

Salad Quartet

Metric/Imperial

1 head of celery
1 × 5 ml spoon/1 teaspoon sesame oil
1 × 15 ml spoon/1 tablespoon soya sauce
1 × 2.5 ml spoon/½ teaspoon salt

20 radishes
1 × 15 ml spoon/1 tablespoon corn oil
0.5 × 15 ml spoon/½ tablespoon wine vinegar

½ cucumber
pinch of ground ginger
1 × 2.5 ml spoon/½ teaspoon salt
3 × 15 ml spoons/3 tablespoons corn oil
1 × 15 ml spoon/1 tablespoon lemon juice

12 fresh or canned asparagus spears
2 × 15 ml spoons/2 tablespoons lemon juice

American

1 head of celery
1 teaspoon sesame oil
1 tablespoon soya sauce
½ teaspoon salt

20 radishes
1 tablespoon corn oil
½ tablespoon wine vinegar

½ cucumber
pinch of ground ginger
½ teaspoon salt
3 tablespoons corn oil
1 tablespoon lemon juice

12 fresh or canned asparagus spears
2 tablespoons lemon juice

Wash the celery and cut it into 2.5 cm/1 inch lengths. Pour boiling water over them, allow to stand for 1 minute, then drain and chill. Mix together the oil, soya sauce and salt and pour it over the celery, tossing well.

Trim the radishes, and soak them in the oil and vinegar.

Peel, seed and finely chop the cucumber. Blend together the ginger, salt, oil and lemon juice. Toss the cucumber in this dressing.

Pour the lemon juice over the asparagus.

Serve all four salads well chilled.

Right: Hawaiian salad

Hawaiian Salad

Metric/Imperial

1 small lettuce
1–2 heads chicory
225 g/8 oz cottage cheese
4 fresh pineapple rings, halved
2 large oranges, peeled and divided into segments
5 cm/2 inch cucumber, thinly sliced

DRESSING:

3 × 15 ml spoons/3 tablespoons corn oil
1 × 15 ml spoon/1 tablespoon lemon juice
salt
freshly ground black pepper
pinch of ground ginger
1 × 2.5 ml spoon/½ teaspoon dry mustard
apple slices to garnish

American

1 small head lettuce
1–2 heads Belgian endive
1 cup cottage cheese
4 fresh pineapple rings, halved
2 large oranges, peeled and divided into segments
2 inch cucumber, thinly sliced

DRESSING:

3 tablespoons corn oil
1 tablespoon lemon juice
salt
freshly ground black pepper
pinch of ground ginger
½ teaspoon dry mustard
apple slices to garnish

Wash the lettuce and shake the leaves dry. Line a serving plate with them. Separate and wash the chicory (Belgian endive) leaves and arrange them at each end of the plate.

Spoon the cottage cheese into the centre, and surround it with borders of pineapple, orange and cucumber.

Whisk together the oil, lemon juice, salt, pepper, ginger and mustard. Dip the apple slices into this dressing to prevent browning and arrange them on top of the cottage cheese.

Serve the remaining dressing apart.

Above: Fruits rich in vitamin C – blackberries, oranges, strawberries, grapefruit and Chinese gooseberries

Desserts

Fresh Fruit Salad

There can be no hard and fast rules for a Fruit Salad. Its content will vary according to the time of year and the state of your finances; but its preparation must always be meticulous. There must be no pips, skin or pith. The fruit must be very fresh and cut, where necessary, into neat, small pieces.

Try to vary not only the colours but the texture of the fruit, including some crisp and some soft fruit.

Toss apple, pear and banana slices in a little lemon juice to prevent them from browning.

Some suggested Fruit Salad combinations
apple, peach, orange and grapes
melon, grapefruit, pear and pineapple
raspberries, pears, apricots and gooseberries
tangerine, banana, apple and bilberries
(blueberries)
strawberries, melon, cherries and apples

Below: Fresh fruit salad

Strawberries

Strawberries are surprisingly – and gratifyingly – low in calories. It is only when you feel the need to sprinkle them with sugar and shroud them in cream that the trouble starts.

Learn some new strawberry habits. In Scotland, where I took to eating my porridge with salt, I learned to eat my strawberries with just a dusting of white pepper. Sceptics can prove for themselves that this really does release the flavour.

Or, try them sprinkled with fresh lemon or orange juice.

Or, make a sauce by puréeing some of the softer, over ripe strawberries together with some raspberries or redcurrants and a little grated orange peel. Serve the more beautiful, whole strawberries on a layer of this and you will not miss the cream.

If you really must have cream with your strawberries, remember that soured cream is less fattening than single (light) cream, and only half as fattening as double (heavy) cream. Eke it out with some stiffly beaten egg white and the damage will be still less.

But best of all, for your waistline's sake, enjoy the strawberries just as Nature intended.

Oven Baked Damsons

Metric/Imperial
0.5 kg/1 lb damsons
1 × 2.5 ml spoon/½ teaspoon cinnamon
juice of 1 orange
rind of 1 orange
2 × 15 ml spoons/2 tablespoons clear honey
1 × 15 ml spoon/1 tablespoon dry vermouth
2 × 15 ml spoons/2 tablespoons water

American
4 cups damsons
½ teaspoon cinnamon
juice of 1 orange
rind of 1 orange
2 tablespoons clear honey
1 tablespoon dry vermouth
2 tablespoons water

Wipe but do not stone (pit) the damsons. Place them in a casserole.

In a saucepan bring to the boil the cinnamon, orange juice, orange rind, honey, vermouth and water.

Pour this over the damsons. Cover with foil and bake in a preheated moderate oven (180°C/350°F, Gas Mark 4) for 30 minutes.

Serve either hot or cold.

This recipe is suitable for any member of the plum family.

Cottage Pears

Metric/Imperial
4 ripe eating pears
1 × 15 ml spoon/1 tablespoon lemon juice
100 g/4 oz cottage cheese, sieved
0.5 × 2.5 ml spoon/¼ teaspoon freshly grated nutmeg
8 strawberries to decorate

American
4 ripe dessert pears
1 tablespoon lemon juice
½ cup cottage cheese, strained
¼ teaspoon freshly grated nutmeg
8 strawberries to decorate

Chill the pears. Peel them if necessary, then halve them lengthwise, discarding any pips or core. Sprinkle the pears with lemon juice.

Blend together the cottage cheese and nutmeg.

Fill each hollowed pear half with the cheese mixture. Top each one with a strawberry.

Tangy Fresh Orange Jelly

Metric/Imperial
3 large oranges
1 lemon
300 ml/½ pint water
15 g/½ oz powdered gelatine
artificial liquid sweetener

American
3 large oranges
1 lemon
1¼ cups water
2 tablespoons powdered gelatin
artificial liquid sweetener

Using a potato peeler, peel the oranges and lemon very thinly, taking care to leave the pith behind. Put the orange and lemon peel in a saucepan with the water, bring to the boil and allow to simmer for 10 minutes.

Put 4 × 15 ml spoons/4 tablespoons cold water in a basin. Sprinkle in the gelatine and allow to soak for 5 minutes. Add this to the pan containing the peel and water, away from the heat, and stir well until completely dissolved. Strain this into a measuring jug, add the strained juice of the oranges and lemon and make up to 600 ml/1 pint (2½ cups), adding cold water if necessary.

Sweeten to taste with artificial liquid sweetener, but keep it tangy. Pour into a moistened jelly mould and chill until set.

Fresh Peaches with Raspberry Sauce

Metric/Imperial
6 ripe peaches
225 g/½ lb raspberries
1 × 15 ml spoon/1 tablespoon clear honey
pinch of cinnamon
1 × 15 ml spoon/1 tablespoon fresh orange juice

American
6 ripe peaches
1½ cups raspberries
1 tablespoon clear honey
pinch of cinnamon
1 tablespoon fresh orange juice

Peel the peaches. If the skins are reluctant to come off, pour boiling water over the peaches, allow to stand for 30 seconds only, then plunge them immediately into cold water. Slice the peeled peaches into a serving bowl and chill.

Rub the raspberries through a nylon sieve (strainer), using a wooden spoon. Blend the honey, cinnamon and orange juice into the raspberry purée. Chill well before pouring over the peaches.

Greek Fruit Salad

Metric/Imperial
2 bananas
1 apple
2 oranges
1 × 15 ml spoon/1 tablespoon dry sherry
250 ml/8 fl oz natural yogurt
2 × 15 ml spoons/2 tablespoons clear honey

American
2 bananas
1 apple
2 oranges
1 tablespoon dry sherry
1 cup unflavored yogurt
2 tablespoons clear honey

Peel the bananas, apple and oranges. Cut all the fruit into very small pieces. Stir in the sherry and allow to stand in a cool place for at least 1 hour.

Whisk together the yogurt and honey. Stir this lightly into the fruit. Chill for a further 1 hour before serving.

Above: A selection of berry fruits with a container of raspberry purée

Melon Balls with Lemon Sauce

Metric/Imperial
1 ripe melon (Honeydew, Charentais, Cantaloup or Ogen)
2 lemons
1 × 15 ml spoon/1 tablespoon sugar
TO GARNISH:
sprigs of mint
lemon slices

American
1 ripe melon (Honeydew, Charentais, Cantaloup or Ogen)
2 lemons
1 tablespoon sugar
TO GARNISH
sprigs of mint
lemon slices

The melon must be absolutely ripe for this dessert. Halve it and remove the seeds. Using a vegetable scoop make as many melon balls as possible. Chill them thoroughly while making the sauce.

Grate the rind of the lemons into a small pan. Squeeze the juice from the two lemons and measure it, adding enough water to make up to 150 ml/¼ pint (⅔ cup). Add this to the rind, together with the sugar and any untidy scraps of melon which remain after the 'balling' process. Bring to the boil and allow to simmer for 5 minutes. Liquidize (blend) this mixture, chill it and put it in the bottom of a glass dish. Top it with the melon balls, mint and lemon slices.

Melon and Grapes

Metric/Imperial
1 small melon (Honeydew, Cantaloup or Rock melon)
juice of 1 lemon
1 small bunch seedless grapes, peeled

American
1 small melon (Honeydew, Cantaloup or Rock melon)
juice of 1 lemon
1 cup seedless grapes, peeled

Remove the skin and seeds carefully from the melon and cut the flesh into neat cubes. Pour the lemon juice over them and toss well.

Mix together the grapes and melon cubes. Chill well before serving.

Melon's powerful aroma will invade all the other food in your refrigerator unless it is covered very securely.

Banana Yogurt

Metric/Imperial
4 very ripe bananas
250 ml/8 fl oz natural yogurt
4 × 5 ml spoons/4 teaspoons clear honey

American
4 very ripe bananas
1 cup unflavored yogurt
4 teaspoons clear honey

Peel and chop the bananas. Liquidize (blend) them together with the yogurt.

Serve this pudding chilled, in individual glasses, topping each one with a swirl of honey.

Left: Melon balls with lemon sauce

70

Above: Melon and grapes

Stuffed Pineapple

Metric/Imperial
2 small pineapples
2 oranges
1 × 15 ml spoon/1 tablespoon finely chopped stem
  ginger

> **American**
> *2 small pineapples*
> *2 oranges*
> *1 tablespoon finely chopped stem*
>   *ginger*

Halve the pineapples lengthwise, leaving any leaves, and scoop out the flesh. A grapefruit knife is useful for this process.

Dice the pineapple flesh. Peel the oranges and divide them into segments, carefully discarding any pips or membrane.

Mix together the pineapple, orange and ginger and fill each hollowed pineapple with this fruit mixture. Serve chilled.

Compôte

Metric/Imperial
50 g/2 oz sugar, or equivalent sugar substitute
150 ml/¼ pint water
1 lemon
juice of 1 orange
1 large cooking apple, peeled, cored and sliced
100 g/4 oz blackberries
100 g/4 oz damsons, stoned
100 g/4 oz black plums, stoned
100 g/4 oz golden plums, stoned

> **American**
> *¼ cup sugar or equivalent sugar*
>   *substitute*
> *⅔ cup water*
> *1 lemon*
> *juice of 1 orange*
> *2 cups peeled, cored and sliced*
>   *baking apple*
> *1 cup blackberries*
> *1 cup damsons, pitted*
> *4 oz black plums, pitted*
> *4 oz golden plums, pitted*

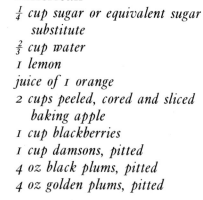

Put the sugar and water in a large thick pan. Add 2 or 3 large pieces of lemon rind and the strained juice of the lemon and the orange.

Bring to the boil, stirring until the sugar has dissolved. Add the apples, blackberries, damsons and plums.

Simmer gently until the fruit is cooked. Remove the lemon rind and serve either hot or cold.

Vary according to whatever fruit is available.

Oranges and Grapes

Metric/Imperial
6 oranges
juice of 1 lemon
rind of ½ lemon
1 × 15 ml spoon/1 tablespoon demerara sugar
few drops vanilla essence
225 g/8 oz black grapes, deseeded

> **American**
> *6 oranges*
> *juice of 1 lemon*
> *rind of ½ lemon*
> *1 tablespoon brown sugar*
> *few drops vanilla extract*
> *2 cups seeded pitted purple grapes*

Peel the oranges with a sharp, serrated knife, taking care to remove all the rind and pith. Slice the oranges across thinly, taking care to catch all the juice.

Put this juice in a small pan, together with the lemon juice. Using a potato peeler or sharp knife, remove the rind from ½ lemon. Add it to the pan, together with the sugar and vanilla essence (extract). Bring to the boil, and allow to cook quickly until well reduced.

Allow to cool, then pour this over the oranges, discarding the lemon rind. Add the grapes and chill before serving.

Pineapple Baskets

This is not so much a recipe as a method of serving fresh pineapple, making it attractive and easy to eat.

Halve the pineapple lengthwise, or, if it is very large, quarter it lengthwise, including the leaves.

Using a very sharp grapefruit knife, penetrate the flesh of the pineapple just underneath the hard centre core. Cut all the way along, then down and along the bottom edge, just inside the prickly skin.

Turn the half pineapple round and do the same at the other side.

When this is done it should be possible to remove all the tender flesh in one piece. But do not do this. Instead, cut it into neat, bite size pieces, but leave it looking like an intact demi-pineapple.

When the pineapple has been eaten you are left with a basket shape which is made up of all the inedible parts of the fruit – the centre core, prickly skin and leaves.

For a special party effect, you could remove just one or two of the cubes of pineapple and replace them with perfect whole strawberries or huge black grapes.

Above: Oranges and grapes

Coeur à la Crême

Metric/Imperial
350 g/12 oz low fat cottage cheese
150 ml/¼ pint natural yogurt
juice of ½ lemon
rind of ½ lemon
2 × 5 ml spoons/2 teaspoons unflavoured gelatine
2 × 15 ml spoons/2 tablespoons warm water
4 × 5 ml spoons/4 teaspoons demerara sugar
cinnamon

American
1½ cups low fat cottage cheese
⅔ cup unflavored yogurt
juice of ½ lemon
rind of ½ lemon
2 teaspoons unflavored gelatin
2 tablespoons warm water
4 teaspoons brown sugar
cinnamon

Using a wooden spoon, press the cottage cheese through a sieve (strainer), into a mixing bowl.

Blend in the yogurt, lemon juice and lemon rind.

Dissolve the gelatine in the warm water. Stir this into the cheese mixture, making sure that it is evenly distributed.

Line individual pierced moulds (heart shaped, if possible) with cheesecloth. Fill each one with the cheese mixture and chill overnight.

Turn them out on to individual plates and sprinkle each one with a spoonful of brown sugar and a dusting of cinnamon.

To show them at their best, serve these pretty heart shaped desserts on brightly coloured plates. Alternatively, line plain white plates with freshly washed blackcurrant leaves or fig leaves.

Summer fruits such as strawberries, raspberries, black currants or Chinese gooseberries (if available) would happily partner Coeur à la Crême, and would provide a dramatic splash of colour as a contrast.

Rhubarb Meringue

Metric/Imperial
0.5 kg/1 lb rhubarb
freshly grated nutmeg
2 × 15 ml spoons/2 tablespoons sugar
3 egg whites
2 × 15 ml spoons/2 tablespoons sifted icing sugar

American
1 lb rhubarb
freshly grated nutmeg
2 tablespoons sugar
3 egg whites
2 tablespoons sifted confectioners'
    sugar

Wipe the rhubarb and cut it into 2.5 cm/1 inch pieces. Put them in a deep casserole and sprinkle them with the nutmeg and sugar.

Whisk the egg whites until they are so stiff that the bowl may be safely turned upside down without them falling out. Carefully fold in the icing (confectioners') sugar.

Pile this meringue on top of the rhubarb and bake in a preheated moderate oven (180°C/350°F, Gas Mark 4) for 30 minutes.

This same 'meringue' treatment may be applied to any other fruit. Try it with plums, a mixture of apple and blackberries, apricots or gooseberries.

Whatever your chosen fruit, remember to whisk the egg whites until they are really stiff. You may find this easier if you chill the egg whites for an hour before whisking, and if you add just a tiny pinch of salt.

Rhubarb and Yogurt Fool

Metric/Imperial
0.5 kg/1 lb rhubarb, washed and cut into
    2.5 cm/1 inch lengths
2 × 15 ml spoons/2 tablespoons demerara sugar
1 × 15 ml spoon/1 tablespoon grated orange peel
1 × 15 ml spoon/1 tablespoon fresh orange juice
pinch of ground ginger
600 ml/1 pint natural yogurt

American
1 lb rhubarb, washed and cut
    into 1 inch lengths
2 tablespoons brown sugar
1 tablespoon grated orange peel
1 tablespoon fresh orange juice
pinch of ground ginger
2½ cups unflavored yogurt

Gently stew the rhubarb with the sugar, orange peel, orange juice and ginger until very soft. Allow it to cool.

Stir in the yogurt, check for sweetness and chill for at least 1 hour before serving.

Above: Rhubarb and yoghurt fool

Poached Apples

Metric/Imperial
4 eating apples
juice of $\frac{1}{2}$ lemon
150 ml/$\frac{1}{4}$ pint fresh orange juice
2 × 15 ml spoons/2 tablespoons water
pinch of ground cinnamon

American
4 dessert apples
juice of $\frac{1}{2}$ lemon
$\frac{2}{3}$ cup fresh orange juice
2 tablespoons water
pinch of ground cinnamon

Peel the apples carefully, without removing the stalks. Roll each apple in lemon juice to prevent browning. Poach them gently in the orange juice and water, flavoured with cinnamon, until cooked but not too soft. A frying pan (skillet) is useful for this process as it allows space for turning the apples without damaging them.

Serve hot or cold.

For a special occasion, flambé the poached apples. Gin is the least calorific of the spirits and you need only 1 × 15 ml spoon/1 tablespoon for quite a spectacular effect. Warm the gin in a soup ladle and ignite it just as you pour it over the hot poached apples.

Apple Slices with Honey

Metric/Imperial
8 eating apples, peeled, cored and sliced
2 cloves
juice of 1 orange
rind of 1 orange
2 × 15 ml spoons/2 tablespoons clear honey
2 × 15 ml spoons/2 tablespoons water

American
6 cups peeled, cored and sliced
*   dessert apples*
2 cloves
juice of 1 orange
rind of 1 orange
2 tablespoons clear honey
2 tablespoons water

Place the apples and cloves in a baking dish.

Mix together the orange juice, orange rind, honey and water.

Pour this over the apples. Cover with foil and bake in a preheated moderate oven (180°C/350°F, Gas Mark 4) for 20 to 25 minutes.

Serve either hot or cold.

Below: Poached apples

Baked Apricots

Metric/Imperial
0.5 kg/1 lb apricots, halved and stoned
1 × 15 ml spoon/1 tablespoon fresh orange juice
25 g/1 oz vanilla sugar*

American
1 lb apricots, halved and pitted
1 tablespoon fresh orange juice
2 tablespoons vanilla sugar

Arrange the apricots in an ovenproof dish. Sprinkle them with the orange juice, then the vanilla sugar.

Bake in a preheated cool oven (140°C/275°F, Gas Mark 1) for 1 hour.

Serve hot or cold.

*Vanilla sugar can be bought in rather expensive small packets, or it can be made at home by storing a vanilla pod in an airtight container of caster sugar. The vanilla pod flavours the sugar and will not need replacing for months. Just fill up with more sugar as it is needed.

Baked Apple with Orange

Metric/Imperial
4 medium cooking apples
2 × 15 ml spoons/2 tablespoons low calorie marmalade
1 × 5 ml spoons/1 teaspoon grated orange rind
2 × 15 ml spoons/2 tablespoons fresh orange juice
thin strips of orange peel to garnish

American
4 medium baking apples
2 tablespoons low calorie marmalade
1 teaspoon grated orange rind
2 tablespoons fresh orange juice
thin strips of orange peel to garnish

Carefully core but do not peel the apples. Make small slits in the top of each apple to prevent the skin from bursting during cooking.

Blend together the marmalade, orange juice and orange rind.

Fill the centre of each apple with this mixture. Bake them in the centre of a preheated moderate oven (180°C/350°F, Gas Mark 4) for 1 hour.

Garnish each baked apple with thin strips of orange peel.

Right: Baked apple with orange

Snowy Apple

Metric/Imperial
50 g/2 oz sugar, or equivalent sugar substitute
150 ml/¼ pint water
0.75 kg/1½ lb cooking apples, peeled cored and sliced
1 egg yolk, beaten
2 egg whites, stiffly beaten
cinnamon

American
4 tablespoons sugar
⅔ cup water
6 cups peeled, cored and sliced apples
1 egg yolk, beaten
2 egg whites, stiffly beaten
cinnamon

Put the sugar and water in a thick pan and heat gently, stirring until the sugar has dissolved. Add the apples and allow to simmer gently until they are very soft.

Liquidize (blend) the apples, or rub them through a sieve (strainer). Allow to cool slightly, then blend in the egg yolk. Mix well and allow to cool completely. Fold in the egg whites.

Transfer the snowy apple to a glass serving dish and top with a sprinkling of cinnamon.

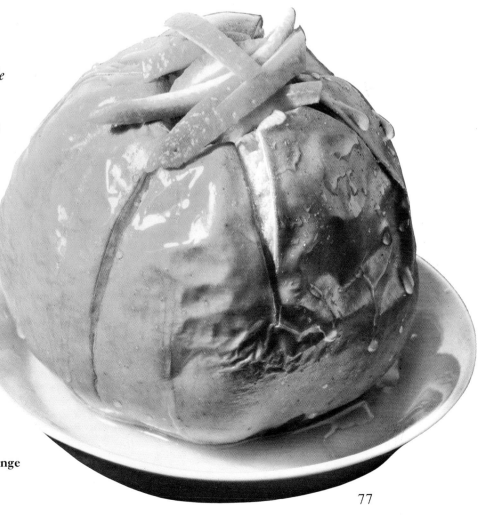

Pink Poached Apples and Pears

Metric/Imperial
0.5 kg/1 lb red fruit, such as stoned plums,
   redcurrants, raspberries, loganberries or
   rhubarb, either a mixture or a single variety
sugar, if needed
2 eating apples
2 eating pears

American
3 cups red fruit, such as pitted
   plums, redcurrants, raspberries, loganberries or
   rhubarb, either a mixture or
   a single variety
sugar, if needed
2 dessert apples
2 dessert pears

Poach the red fruit gently in very little water, with sugar if a sour fruit is chosen. Cook until quite soft then liquidize (blend). Check for sweetness.

Peel the apples and pears carefully, without removing the stalks. Gently poach them in the red purée until cooked but not too soft.

Serve either hot or cold.

Below: Pink poached apples and pears

West Country Pears

Metric/Imperial
300 ml/½ pint dry cider
2 strips lemon peel
1 stick of cinnamon, or
   0.5 × 2.5 ml spoon/¼ teaspoon ground
   cinnamon
few drops of cochineal (optional)
4 eating pears

American
1¼ cups dry hard cider
2 strips lemon peel
1 stick of cinnamon, or
   ¼ teaspoon ground cinnamon
few drops of cochineal (optional)
4 dessert pears

Place the cider, lemon rind, cinnamon and cochineal in a pan. Bring to the boil, cover and boil for 1 minute.

Peel the pears carefully, without removing the stalks. Stand them upright in a casserole dish, cutting a thin slice from the base of any pear which threatens to fall over.

Pour over the cider, cover and cook in a preheated moderate oven (180°C/350°F, Gas Mark 4) for 30 to 40 minutes, basting from time to time.

Carefully transfer the cooked pears to a serving dish, and strain the liquid over them.

Serve hot or cold.

Above: West country pears

Index

American salad 60
Apple:
  Apple slices with honey 76
  Baked apple with orange 75
  Pink poached apples and pears 78
  Poached apples 76
  Snowy apples 75
Apricots, baked 75
Aubergines (Eggplants), stuffed 49

Bacon joints, boiled 32
Banana yogurt 70
Beef:
  Beef with cabbage 17
  Boiled salt beef brisket or ox (beef) tongue 20
  Cold baked silverside (brisket) of beef 20
  French country casserole 19
  Pepper steak 19
  Roast beef 17
  Slimmers Stroganoff 18
Bortsch 13

Cabbage:
  Beef with cabbage 17
  Cabbage with sweet and sour sauce 57
  Danish red cabbage 54
  Stuffed cabbage leaves 50
Carrot and watercress soup 11
Cauliflower:
  Cauliflower with tomato sauce 57
  Italian cauliflower salad 61
Celery, braised 57
Chicken:
  Chicken with bacon and mushrooms 26
  Chicken and peach salad 28
  Chicken with peppers 27
  Chicken Veronica 26
  Coq à l'orange 29
  Devilled chicken legs 30
  Ham and chicken mould 33
  Spanish chicken 29
Coeur à la crème 74
Compôte 72
Cottage cheese dip 6
Cottage cheese and ham bake 6
Cucumber salad with yogurt 62
Curried haddock mousse 41

Damsons, oven baked 68
Desserts 67–79
Devilled chicken legs 30
Dip, cottage cheese 6

Fenouil à la grecque 52
Fish:
  To fillet fish 37
  Chinese braised fish 45
  Fisherman's stew 41
  Leftover fish 42
  Lemony fish 39
  Somerset fish 38
  Summer fish 44
  Summer fish with orange 45
Flounder see Plaice
French beans with garlic and herbs 54
French country casserole 19
Fruit. See also Apple etc.
  Compôte 72
  Fresh fruit salad 67
  Greek fruit salad 69

Gammon steaks with orange sauce 32
Grape:
  Melon and grapes 70
  Orange and grapes 72
Greek fruit salad 69
Greek salata 62

Haddock mousse, curried 41
Halibut, shrimp and, salad 39
Ham:
  boiled ham joints 32
  Cottage cheese and ham bake 6
  Ham and chicken mould 33
  Melon with smoked ham 9
Hawaiian salad 65
Herring:
  Normandy herrings 8
  Soused herrings 42
Hors d'oeuvre 5–9

Kidneys, Chinese 34

Lamb:
  Lamb casserole with orange 24
  Lamb shish kebabs with herbs 23
  Spiced simmered leg of lamb 22
Leek:
  Leeks with tomato sauce 54
  Liver and leeks 35
Lemon:
  Lemon dressing 60
  Lemony fish 39
  Melon balls with lemon sauce 70
Liver and leeks 35

Meat and poultry 17–35
  See also Beef etc.
Melon:
  Melon balls with lemon sauce 70
  Melon and grapes 70
  Melon with smoked ham 9
Minestrone 12
Mushroom:
  Chicken with bacon and mushrooms 26
  Mushroom salad 9
  Mushroom sauce 40
  Mushroom and tomatoes 52
  Raw mushrooms with lemon dressing 60
  Steamed trout with mushrooms and shrimps 38
  Tomato and mushroom vinaigrette 5

Orange:
  Baked apple with orange 75
  Coq à l'orange 29
  Lamb casserole with orange 24
  Orange and watercress salad 64
  Orange and grapes 72
  Oranges and grapes 72
  Summer fish with orange 45
  Tangy fresh orange jelly 68

Peaches, fresh, with raspberry sauce 69
Pear:
  Cottage pears 69
  Pink poached apples and pears 78
  West country pears 78
Pepper steak 19
Peppers:
  Chicken with peppers 27
  Pepper and olive salad 60
  Sea scallops with peppers 92
Pineapple:
  Pineapple baskets 72
  Stuffed pineapple 72
Plaice with mushroom sauce 40
Pork chops with lemon and ginger 32
Prawn (shrimp) and egg flower soup 32

Raspberry sauce, fresh peaches with 69
Ratatouille 52
Red cabbage, Danish 54
Rhubarb meringue 74
Rhubarb and yogurt fool 74

Salads 9, 28, 39, 59–65
Scallops with peppers 44
Shrimp and halibut salad 39
Soups 11–15
Soused herrings 42
Strawberries 68
Stroganoff for slimmers 18
Summer soup, chilled 14
Swedes, purée of 50
Sweet and sour sauce 57

Tomato:
  Chilled tomato soup 11
  Mushrooms and tomatoes 52
  Stuffed tomatoes 50
  Tomato and mushroom vinaigrette 5
  Tomato salad 62
Tongue, boiled ox (beef) 20

Trout:
  Somerset fish 38
  Steamed trout with mushrooms and shrimps 38
Tuna:
  Thon à la provençale 42
Turkey 31

Veal escalopes 24
Vegetables 49–57. See also Salads
  Raw vegetables with cottage cheese dip 6

Watermelon soup 15

Yogurt:
  Banana yogurt 70
  Cucumber salad with yogurt 62
  Rhubarb and yogurt fool 74

ACKNOWLEDGEMENTS

The publishers would like to thank the following organizations and individuals for their kind permission to reproduce the photographs in this book:

Bryce Attwell 40 56; Rex Bamber contents page; Birds Eye 19, 26; Brown and Polson 27; Eden Vale Ltd. 5, 6, 65; Fruit Producer's Council 28; Melvin Grey 69; Herring Industry Board 37, 38; Paul Kemp 34; Lawry's Foods Incorporated 18; John Lee 20, 23, 33, 44, 64, 70; Neil Lorrimer 22; National Magazines 48; 'New Idea' Magazine 51; Norman Nicholls title page, 7, 13, 30, 36, 53, 55, 58, 66, 71, 75, 79; Octopus Books 8, 53, 61, 63; Roger Phillips endpapers; Photopad 12; R.H.M. Foods Ltd. 4; Syndication International 14, 29, 31, 39, 77; Tabasco Sauce 25; Patrick Yapp 35, 78.